SAVING STATE U

SAVING STATE U

Why We Must Fix Public Higher Education

Nancy Folbre

THE NEW PRESS

NEW YORK
LONDON

Requests for permission to reproduce selections from this book should be mailed to:
Permissions Department, The New Press, 38 Greene Street, New York, NY 10013.

Published in the United States by The New Press, New York, 2010
Distributed by Perseus Distribution

LIBRARY OF CONGRESS CATALOGING-IN-PUBLICATION DATA
Folbre, Nancy.
    Saving State U: why we must fix public higher education / Nancy Folbre.
       p.   cm.
    Includes bibliographical references.
    ISBN 978-1-59558-065-8 (hc.: alk. paper)   1. State universities and colleges—
United States.   2. Educational change—United States.   I. Title.
    LB2329.5F65 2010
    378'.050973—dc22   2009034020

The New Press was established in 1990 as a not-for-profit alternative to the large,
commercial publishing houses currently dominating the book publishing industry.
The New Press operates in the public interest rather than for private gain, and is
committed to publishing, in innovative ways, works of educational, cultural, and
community value that are often deemed insufficiently profitable.

www.thenewpress.com

Composition by dix!
This book was set in Bembo

Printed in the United States of America

10 9 8 7 6 5 4 3 2 1

CONTENTS

ACKNOWLEDGMENTS

André Schiffrin inspired this book. Ellen Reeves, Jennifer Rappaport, Ellen Adler, and many other hardworking staff at The New Press helped move it forward. Hugh Corr provided excellent research assistance. My colleagues Dan Clawson and Max Page gave me helpful feedback. They, along with other members of the Public Higher Education Network of Massachusetts (PHENOM), set an extraordinary example of commitment to the cause of public higher education. Thanks to all.

SAVING STATE U

INTRODUCTION

You Mass, I Mass, we all Mass at UMass.
—Bathroom graffiti, Thompson Hall

The patchwork, make-do, halfhearted system we have for partially subsidizing higher education in the United States is both inefficient and unfair. I have been worried about it for the last twenty-eight years, while teaching economics at the University of Massachusetts at Amherst. This book represents my best effort to make sense of my worries. While it grows out of my personal experience at one institution, it speaks to the experience of all state universities and addresses a momentous national issue. It explains why we need free public higher education in the United States and how we should pay for it.

State universities cannot be saved in isolation. They sink or swim with a revitalized vision of social democracy, an economic system based on commitments to the development of human capabilities. Saving public higher education can help us sustain the social contract on which a competitive market economy must be based. It can offer citizens a way to reaffirm their faith in principles of equal opportunity. And it can give taxpayers a better understanding of what they get in return for what they pay. In this book, I will explore these possibilities.

Almost all teachers have experienced variations on the basic nightmare: the one in which you have lost your notes and can't find your way to class. My waking experiences have been consistently worse, more like trying to teach under water: so much energy goes into our efforts just to catch our necessary breaths. Those of us who teach at public colleges and universities have swum through a period of weakened societal commitment to public higher education and steady deterioration in the quality of its undergraduate programs. Worst of all is the gradual demoralization that diminishes everybody's expectations.

The election of President Barack Obama in 2008 offered the possibility of a turnaround. He spoke eloquently of the need to increase our commitment to public higher education. He set an ambitious goal: that the population of the United States should achieve the highest proportion of college graduates in the world by 2020.[1] He followed through with an ambitious fiscal stimulus that significantly increased financial aid and transferred federal funds to the states to protect public universities from budget cuts. He reformed the student loan system.

But the economy itself, which began to tank almost a year before Obama was elected, continued to lose oxygen. By June 2009 the stock market had rebounded significantly but unemployment remained painfully high at 9.5 percent. State revenues were collapsing. The state of California was so broke that it resorted to paying some of its bills with IOUs. A concerted campaign to reform the nation's health-care industry was underway, with much attention to how much it would cost and who would pay. Many public universities were threatening layoffs, freezing hiring, and raising student fees.

At first glance, it didn't seem like a good time to demand more support for public higher education. On the other hand, the economic crisis highlighted a larger set of misplaced priorities. The federal government committed $12.2 trillion to bail out failing financial institutions;[2] CNN calculated about $835 billion spent by mid-2009.[3] Let's put that number in context. States spent about $85 billion on their public colleges and universities in 2008—not much more than 10 percent of the total mid-2009 bailout figure.[4] As of June 30, 2009, the National Student Loan Debt Clock that flashes at the Student Debt Alert Web site registered $584.5 billion.[5] That's less than 5 percent of the total bailout commitment. The current economic crisis makes us seem pretty small. So why are we suffocating? Could it be that it's our own fault, that we've just been holding our breath too long?

Back in 2000, our slogan was Save UMass, a phrase that evoked a more general piece of advice: Save Your Rear End. The slogan grew out of efforts by faculty, staff, and students to lobby the Massachusetts state legislature to increase funding for its public university system. To an expatriate Texan like myself, the need for this effort seemed pretty weird. The Commonwealth of Massachusetts, once known as Taxachusetts, is supposedly the most liberal state in the country. If voters wouldn't support high-quality public higher education here, where on earth would they? Maybe social democracy—or, as the Other Side puts it, the Nanny State—was drowning in the bathtub.

In that year, my university, along with the rest of the world, was losing confidence in the very concept of a commonwealth. George W. Bush was moving into the White House, and, soon after, Mitt Romney settled into our governor's mansion. Both brandished their credentials as businessmen and their confidence in the private sector. Both declared that public spending was inefficient and tax increases were evil. The new chancellor of the UMass Amherst campus embraced a popular new business-model approach to university management: watch us cut costs! Whack, whack whack.

The sharp recession of 2001–2002 reduced tax revenues in most states, revenues that were already on the decline as a result of tax cuts. Cuts to our UMass Amherst budget were part of this national trend. I was the acting chairperson of the Department of Economics at the time and could see exactly how those cuts were reducing the quality of the services we offered. In addition, the better part of my own higher education was paid for by the taxpayers of Texas and Massachusetts, who certainly deserved their money's worth. It occurred to me that I might take a break from a long-term effort to understand the laws of motion of economic systems and turn my attention to something slightly more . . . immediate.

So there I was, one buttery autumn day before the leaves had started to turn, leafleting parents as they helped their children move into the Orchard Hill dorm. The handout composed by the faculty union explained the probable effects of the budget cuts and urged citizens to lobby their state representatives on behalf of the university. I had a hard time finding anyone who would read it. The last thing parents wanted to hear as they helped load suitcases, computers, and stuffed animals into the elevator was a warning that it might come to a grinding halt.

I then delivered a lecture on the costs and benefits of the Great Elevator of Upward Mobility that I, as a college educator, personally help operate: in today's labor market, young people unable to brandish a college degree are largely doomed to economic insecurity, if not outright poverty. About 74 percent of college students in the country attend public institutions that, like mine, depend upon the informed support of a taxpaying electorate. That support is not merely slipping away; it is being hammered down, peeled off, and chopped up by political and budgetary warfare. States are reducing their subsidies for public higher education. As a result, the price to students and their parents is being ratcheted up. For families in the exact middle of the income distribution—the third quintile—average net college costs at public four-year colleges and universities increased from about 18 percent to about 25 percent of median family income between 1999 and 2007.[6]

The ratchet is embedded within the very structure of state government finance. Public investment in higher education is discretionary, a fancy word for "We'll do whatever we can with whatever is left over." Commitments to entitlements such as K–12 education, health insurance for the poor, and benefits and pensions for state employees are inscribed in law. As the costs of these programs go up, expenditures must follow. Meanwhile, state revenues grow much more slowly. Proposals to increase those revenues by hiking taxes meet not only with strenuous opposition but with an explicit threat: raise taxes and you will drive both businesses and high-income residents from the state.

This threat, typically uttered with great conviction, was frequently accompanied by strong claims about what voters really want: they don't want to pay higher taxes; they don't want to expand public services. This refrain appeared over and over in the newspaper, on the radio, on the television. It was like the music that plays when you are put on hold. The voice was disembodied and impossible to argue with. All you could do, really, was hang up on it.

I could hear it, even at the dorm. When I ran out of leaflets, I seemed to lose my ability to speak. I wasn't sure I could explain my worries to students or their parents.

I knew more about the general economics of education than the specifics of my own institution. I had no idea what students and their families were paying for tuition and fees, much less how a budget cut would affect the average undergraduate.

I didn't understand the state budget, either. None of my formal training in economics included coursework in public finance. Even if it had, I'm not sure it would have helped me much. The budget, though available online, seemed written in a language all its own. Although I had been paying taxes in the state for years, I could not figure out how total revenues were raised or spent. *Boston Globe* reporting dramatized the personalities rather than the priorities of state legislators. The corrupt renovation of Boston highways known as the Big Dig got more column inches than UMass ever did.

Most of the books I'd read about the so-called crisis of

higher education scolded the institutions of the Ivy League, and with good reason. Once upon a time, they offered substantial need-based aid, ensuring that students from low-income families could attend. Now, they seek to attract the students with the highest test scores to verify their status.

Children of alumni and top athletes enjoy greater preference than members of racial/ethnic or class minorities. Although such travesties symbolize an appalling retreat from the ideals of equal opportunity, they affect only the tiny fraction of college students who attend name-brand schools.

The problems of public higher education are more far-reaching. Community colleges and state universities like UMass Amherst still offer many students a good deal for their money. But because tuition and fees are increasing as a result of decreased public support, what you buy into as a freshman will likely cost more as a sophomore, and still more as a junior or a senior. Low-income students, as well as immigrants, African Americans, and Latinos, are further underrepresented. Students from middle-income families, who typically borrow money to pay their bills, suffer under the weight of the resulting debt, which influences their personal and professional choices for years to come.

Expenses themselves are much easier to measure than the quality of what they buy. State universities are the factories of higher education, designed to capitalize on economies of scale: it's the same lecture, isn't it, whether delivered to 20 students or 200? But the lecture is the least of it, which helps explain why so many students, once enrolled, fall by the wayside. The average six-year graduation rate at state universities is below

60 percent. I have taught a lecture course called Introduction to Microeconomics to a class of more than 200 students about 10 times. More than 15 percent of my students have dropped out or failed primarily because they stopped attending class. It's hard to reach out to them when I can't connect their faces with their names.

In the years since I first leafleted at Orchard Hill, many important reports on the problems of public higher education have been published; I will discuss some of them here. Facts and figures, costs and assessments, trends and projections are my stock in trade. But my primary goal is to explain how public higher education fits into the bigger picture, to explain the strings that tie it to our understanding of global capitalism. And, I will argue, the strings work both ways: students, teachers, and administrators at public institutions are not mere puppets. We need to push and tug.

We can begin by challenging the claim that we just can't afford to provide high-quality public higher education for everyone willing and able to take advantage of it. We can explain how disagreements over educational funding often reflect political conflicts that are complicated and confounded by a misunderstanding of our existing tax system. We can make a stronger case for more progressive taxes to support more generous and effective investments in the younger generation.

Public higher education produces more than just diplomas—certificates of human capital with a high payoff in the private market. It develops broader capabilities that students deploy as citizens, friends, partners, and parents. It nurtures hope, curiosity, confidence, diligence, and care. The value of this output will never be fully captured by measures of future earnings. Like the value of our ecosystem and our legacy of human knowledge, human capabilities surpass the metric of the market. Their development helps us find what Abraham Lincoln called "the better angels of our nature."

1

THE BIG DEAL

From my eighth-floor office in Thompson Hall I can see the history of the U.S. economy: on the northern horizon, Mt. Toby's woods full of deer and turkey; west, toward the Connecticut River, open fields of hay, tobacco leaf, and cucumbers; across the parking lot, a coal-fired electricity plant with picture-book smokestacks; in the foreground, the education industry itself, pulsing with students. Mostly I look at my computer screen. We have gone from hunting and gathering to growing our own food, making our own things, and specializing in services. Now, in the information economy, we're hunter-gatherers again, Googling for a living.

The vast stock of common knowledge now available for free online reminds us that individual transactions—the buying and selling that goes on in markets—represent only a small share of our true economy. Right now, public higher education is part of a collective deal we offer the younger generation. We taxpayers fund K–12 education and require most kids under the age of eighteen to attend school (age cutoffs vary by state). If students study hard, successfully graduate from high school, and give college a try, we partially subsidize the cost for them in a variety of ways. We then expect them to contribute, in turn, to the public good. And because we will tax some share of their earnings as adults to help support us in our old age through Social Security and Medicare, we get paid back.

Such intergenerational transfers are central to our social contract—part of what I call the Big Deal. The payback is more implicit than explicit. You can't exactly follow the money as if it were in your retirement account (the mutual fund, in this case, is metaphorical). Also, both pay and payback vary across individuals and groups; some get more than others, regardless of their age. The Big Deal has other components, including safety nets for financial institutions, health insurance (of one kind or another—for many adults, only minimal emergency care), environmental regulation, and so on.

The Big Deal is a big bone of contention. The rich and powerful constantly hustle to expand their own opportunities. Recent global trends make it easier for them to escape the constraints of the democratic nation-state. While Americans embrace the principle of equal opportunity, many remain uncomfortable with its actual practice. But surely the better we understand the changing dimensions of the Big Deal, the better equipped we are to renegotiate it.

PLAYING GAMES

Imagine that you are an eighteen-year-old applying to college and you know exactly what you want and who you want to be. You will now undertake something like a four-year adventure in the woods and could begin by looking at your trusty map and compass. Alternatively, you could think of this process as a board game like the ones that many colleges now market, something like *Monopoly*. I think of it as *UMass: The Game*).

You start out with some assets, advance according to a roll of the dice, but then exercise some choice and skill regarding what properties to acquire.

Your job is to complete the game, enjoy the process, and make some money when you're done. Part of my job is to help you do so. But it's worthwhile to study the game itself. How many individuals make it through, and what determines their chances of success? The statistics remind me of a famous graphical depiction of Napoleon's army, dwindling steadily as it met subzero weather and increased resistance in its forays to the east. Here's the current prediction: for every 100 public high school ninth-graders nationally, only 69 will graduate from high school four years later, only thirty-nine will enter college the fall after they graduate, only twenty-seven will return to their college for sophomore year, and only eighteen of those original one hundred will earn associate degrees within three years of enrolling in college or bachelor's degrees within six years.[1]

From this vantage point, the game seems less amusing, but the metaphor remains instructive. A new wave of social scientific research models individual behavior in terms of games. Some games are played by individuals, some by teams; some have only two players, some have a large number. Most team-based games require cooperation as well as competition. Sometimes their rules are informal and compliance with them is entirely voluntary. Many games are highly structured, with strict mechanisms for rule enforcement.

Free-market enthusiasts often rail at regulation, but serious competitors always rely on it. In major league baseball, with a maximum of thirteen players on the field, four umpires supervise. In professional basketball, with ten players on the court, three referees can blow a whistle. At the highest level of American football, the twenty-two players on the field are governed by a referee, an umpire, a head linesman, a line judge, a field judge, a side judge, and a back judge. In all three sports, the ratio of direct enforcers to players is roughly one to three—not counting the indirect enforcers who write the rules, hear the appeals, and administer the punishments and fines.

Big businesses can't regulate themselves any more than professional football players can. That's why we set up umpires and design sanctions. The Securities and Exchange Commission (SEC) tries to prevent fraudulent accounting. The Environmental Protection Agency (EPA) tries to prevent pollution. State boards of education and accreditation agencies try to monitor colleges and universities to make sure they don't just sell diplomas. Here again, indirect enforcers come into play.

Economic games are more complex and consequential than the ones we play just for fun. They have so many different layers. *UMass: The Game* is embedded in *Higher Education: The Game*, which is embedded in *The U.S. Economy: The Game*, which is embedded in *Globalization: The Game*. Most people are just worrying about how to play and looking for advice on how to win, and that is hard enough. But along the way you might begin to wonder: Who designed these games? Who gets to set the rules?

GAMES AND WARS

"Game" is a disarming term for what Sun Tzu called the "art of war." Yet war also serves as a threat within a peaceful game, an inducement to cooperate. As Thomas Hobbes observed about three centuries ago, if everybody spends all their time fighting with everyone else, nobody can get much done. People make rules about who should get what and why, and even when these rules are clumsy, stupid, and unfair, they are often better than no rules at all. Universal agreement is not implied. Often enough, might makes right.

The art of war has a long history. My university inhabits a town named after Sir Jeffrey Amherst, British commander-in-chief during the French and Indian War and a famous pioneer of biological warfare. He ordered dissemination among Native Americans of blankets used by the afflicted in a Boston smallpox epidemic, as well as use of "every other method that can serve to Extirpate this Execrable Race."[2] People sometimes mention this extirpation ruefully, in passing, and wonder to themselves about the larger loss.

You can always find it in the background. The UMass class of 1950 commissioned a bronze statue of a warrior named Metawampe with a feather in his hair and a musket in his hands, labeled "the legendary spirit of the red man." Hidden behind a bank of rhododendrons, repaired and repositioned after student pranksters carried him off one year and dumped him in the road, Metawampe is harder to find than the more prominent statue of a Minuteman, the now-official symbol of the university. But the so-called red man is the more memorable sculpture. His slim figure reminds me of Peter Pan. For all we know, Metawampe, if he had gained the upper hand, would have behaved just as badly as Lord Jeff. But the temptation to believe that the world is just and that people, in the end, get what they deserve, is just as dangerous as the impulse to blame ourselves for all injustice. Both emotional extremes impede efforts to understand how group conflict operates. To paraphrase Marx and Engels: the point is not merely to understand conflict, but to reduce it. To challenge Marx and Engels: forms of conflict are not based on class alone, much less on the simplistic opposition between capitalists and workers that their theory relied so heavily upon. Team sports provide a good metaphor for most forms of economic competition. Individuals move among teams and their individual performance matters. But they can win only by being on the winning team.

In society we are aligned with those who seem to be like us and divided into groups—U.S. citizens or not (or not yet), rich or poor, college-educated or not. On a more primal level, it matters whether we are men or women, young or old, parents or childless (or, alternatively, child free). Our alliances lay claims and cut deals. Individuals also do some bargaining on their own, deciding how to group themselves. Then, at some point, loyalties lock in, and we root for our team even if it seems doomed to lose. We do what we can to help it win. When you're playing many games at once, it's hard to keep them straight, much less consider how you might want to change the rules. But this is exactly what higher education should help us do.

THE COMMONS

The commons are spaces, resources, and relationships that we do not privately own. Examples: green spaces that were once common grazing grounds; national parks; the air we breathe; our oceans, our fish, our climate; our cultural and technical knowledge; our friends, families, and communities—each of whose very existence gives us pleasure and hope. The commons are the Web writ large, extended beyond the confines of cyberspace. The commons represent the board on which all our games are played.

Both real and imaginary games require capital—a stock of resources that can yield a flow of future services. To play online you need a computer and a fast connection. Many athletes need stadiums, funds to live on, appropriate equipment, and time to train. Students need schools. Workers need skills. Investors need money to invest. But think about the larger game. Planet Earth is a stock of common capital, subject to depreciation. Human technology, knowledge, and culture are forms of common capital, inherited from the past.

Individuals can own and control land, but ecosystems are the more important asset—they provide services such as pollination, clean air, a stable climate. Even a conservative estimate of the market value of these "ecoservices" far exceeds the annual gross domestic product of the United States.[3] Copyrights and patents allow individuals to capture part of the benefits that they create, but only in a limited and temporary way. Scientific research generates largely public benefits; so too do literature, art, dance, and music. The amount that today's consumers are willing to pay for these represents but a small portion of their value because they last so long, with such un-predictable effects on future innovation and inspiration.

We humans create another form of common capital: our children and ourselves. Without the flesh and bones and brains (the hardware and the software) of our population, we can't take advantage of nature's resources or our own. Some aspects of human capital are the results of individual investment, and parts of the return on capital are privately owned. For example, you may borrow money to go to college, and earn more money as a result. However, individual benefits (in this case, of education) usually spill over to others. Parents spend time and money raising children expecting emotional (not economic) payback. Taxpayers finance public education and in return expect a share of what future workers will produce.

Child rearing and formal education are like ecoservices. The interactions among the parts create a whole more valuable than the sum of all individuals. As with networked comput-ers, the connections enhance the capabilities of the system as a whole. You know people willing to help you out in return for your willingness to help them. The quantity and quality of connections among individuals is sometimes referred to as social capital. As with human capital, individual choice comes into play: you can decide which relationships to invest in. But social capital also has a public dimension. Some families, neighborhoods, and communities make it easier for individu-als to be productive.[4]

The Big Deal includes the rules applied to all the games we play, but most importantly to the assets that cannot be owned.

It's a social contract of sorts, but one less clearly specified than any constitution, extending beyond any one nation-state. It's dynamic and unstable, modified by technological change and shifting balances of power. Sometimes it seems like we players understand it about as well as racehorses understand the Triple Crown. In software terms the Big Deal is the source code, the stuff behind the interface. To understand exactly how it works we need to educate ourselves.

HUMAN CAPITAL

Over the last two centuries the Big Deal has changed in many profound ways. Most obviously, we have figured out how to combine natural assets and human knowledge in ways that offer the potential to meet all our basic needs. John Maynard Keynes called this imaginary endstate "economic bliss." [5] We haven't reached it yet, and perhaps we never will. But changes in the way we raise and educate children have altered the Big Deal. We've moved from a family-oriented system based on high fertility to one based on low fertility—from quantity to quality of life. We've also moved from small, informal schools to vast, state-based formal systems that partially collectivize investments in our children. [6]

The term "human capital," first systematically applied by the English economist Alfred Marshall, became a twentieth-century catchword. Ted Schultz emphasized its contributions to economic development, while Gary Becker devised a more formal theoretical model. [7] Both men won Nobel Prizes for their work (Schultz in 1979, Becker in 1992), and both noted important differences between human and other forms of capital, paying particular attention to the role that government should play.

Education offers an economic payoff (more on this in chapter 4) but that doesn't explain why a citizenry (as opposed to a family or an individual) should invest in it. If it's such a great deal, why shouldn't young people pay for it themselves? In principle, the higher earnings they will receive should enable them to pay off loans and then some. One hitch with this idea is that it's difficult to borrow money without collateral—something most college students lack. And because we have outlawed both slavery and indentured servitude, individuals can't sign away rights to their future earnings.

The solution to this problem seems like an easy one: the government can step in to provide or guarantee such loans. The U.S. government has done this on terms quite lucrative for private lenders. But its guarantees don't provide adequate support for education. Individuals who make the ideal investment based on their personal rate of return to education don't take the benefits to others into account. And the public benefits are profound. Highly educated people are more productive if they work with others who are highly educated. That's one reason why we call education a public good.

The benefits reach well beyond the market economy. All else being equal, more education increases the probability that an individual will participate in political life, stay healthy, volunteer to help others, enjoy a stable marriage, and be an effective parent. When polled in 2006, 84 percent of Americans said they believed that investing in colleges and universities today would help solve future problems.[8] Education also has intrinsic merit, as Aristotle observed long ago.[9] What's the economy for, anyway, if not to create science and make art?

Pension programs such as Social Security are called "pay-as-you-go" because the money being paid in by the working-age generation is being spent on the older generation. It's a good contract between generations, much like the earlier traditional contract in which parents raised children and expected those children to care for them in old age. Our modern contract is a better one, for several reasons. The risk of misfortune is more evenly shared: parents who outlive their children are provided for. Likewise, investment in the younger generation is more evenly spread—even children from the poorest families have some opportunity to get an education. Equality of opportunity makes players in the game try harder because they all have a chance to win.

Pension systems can link the fate of old and young and create solidarity based on reciprocity.[10] On the other hand, they can also create conflicts. While there are benefits to pooling risk, there are also costs, especially for those who think they could fare better on their own. Rich people might prefer to save for their own old age alone, just as healthy people might like to exclude those who are sick from their insurance pool. Inequalities within nations as well as opportunities to move easily among them make such long-term contracts harder to enforce.

HUMAN CAPITAL AND COMPETITION

It's always better to confront conflicts directly than to pretend they don't exist. Critical thinking also sometimes requires a dose of cynicism. Advocates of increased public spending on higher education often describe it as a win-win situation: college graduates will earn more, the United States will become more competitive, and our GDP will grow. It's obvious! A no-brainer! The best salesmen always use this rhetoric, and sometimes it's even true. But if it were so simple, our state universities would be booming.

Human capital may not be purely private, but it's not completely public either. It's created by mixed motives: parental altruism, public commitments, moral obligations, individual affinities and desires for gain, and differing groups forming coalitions to pursue all of the above. The best strategy is seldom clear, especially as support for public higher education cycles up and down. As with many deals, the devil is in the details.

Increases in educational levels don't benefit everybody equally. Most of us sell our human capital services for a wage, and, all else being equal, as the supply of those services increases, the price paid for them goes down. I've been teaching about the forces of supply and demand for thirty years, and there's one question introductory economics texts ignore: how much exactly do we want to increase that supply? If everyone goes to college, the market value of a college degree could more easily decline.

Recently, I told students at Keene State College in New Hampshire that they deserved free tuition and fees. Since most of them are hustling hard to put themselves through school, you'd think that they would favor this, and they did. But the suggestion made them anxious. As one student put it, "somebody has to pull the lattes." No one understands this better than someone who has faced the possibility of a lifetime behind a Starbucks counter. The calculus of costs and benefits here is much harder than adding five and subtracting two. No one knows the functional form.

Uncertainty strengthens the impulse to stick together and compete as a team. Most team memberships are not chosen but assigned. Most U.S. citizens are born, not made. Within the Big Team, also known as the nation-state, social and economic divisions determine access to education as well as ability to make good use of it. Many histories of education point to the role of special interests and political elites.[11] But the impact of group identity reaches beyond fragmentation at the top, encompassing loyalties based on race and gender as well as class.

No conspiracies are needed for this story, or calculations of collective gain. Loyalties simply become alignments that change perceptions of both identity and interests, like family ties. Many efforts to increase educational spending are local ones—campaigning for higher taxes in your own school district, lobbying for your own state university, donating to your alma mater. Competition among teams can be healthy and innocuous—except, of course, when it is not.

Histories of inequality offer us important lessons. In the early nineteenth century, spokesmen for Great Britain's upper class openly opposed education for the "laboring classes" on the grounds that it would "teach them to despise their lot in life, instead of making them good servants in agriculture."[12] In the New World, the countries of South America, dominated by small landlord elites, declined to pay taxes to educate the masses.[13] In the United States, few plantation owners in the antebellum South saw benefits to educating their slaves, who were set to work primarily in the fields. There were, of course, exceptions, particularly in urban areas. Slaves who gained literacy and business skills become more productive and therefore more profitable assets. But after 1830 even those who might have wanted to educate their slaves were prohibited by law. The fear of slave rebellion had become too great.

In the wake of the Civil War, the North's occupation of the South (known as Reconstruction) brought black children into schools. Whether because of cultural inertia or fear of economic competition, whites soon established manipulative forms of segregation through what were known as Jim Crow laws. The separate schools established as a result were inferior in every way to those provided for white children.[14] Employers may well have benefited from racial divisions among workers, but white workers themselves gained a superior access to education that helped them protect their dominant position.[15]

Residential segregation intensifies inequalities based on class as well as race and ethnicity. Primary and secondary schools in the United States have long been financed by local property taxes. Rich neighborhoods can fund good schools, and good schools can make the neighborhood even richer. Poor neighborhoods lack the starter capital (in both financial and human form) to bootstrap their schools into this virtuous circle. Children living in poor neighborhoods have few opportunities to engage with highly educated people.

Throughout most of the nineteenth century, young girls were welcomed into elementary schools as generously as young boys. But female attendance in secondary schools was often restricted, and college education for women was explicitly discouraged. Among the many fears expressed was the possibility that women with opportunities outside the home would neglect their wifely duties. Alfred Marshall famously argued that women should not be allowed to pursue graduate degrees in economics because their obligations to their little units of baby human capital should come first.

Resistance to expanding public education has never been based on ignorance alone. The historical track record suggests that individuals have consciously or unconsciously aligned themselves into teams in an effort to protect or enhance their own team's advantage. Thus public investment in education is shaped not just by the level of benefits relative to costs, but also by how those benefits are distributed and captured. Also relevant, of course, are team efforts to evade costs. This game of strategy makes World of Warcraft truly seem like child's play.

PRESSURES ON THE WELFARE STATE

Government spending on education, health, and social insurance—the programs often dubbed "the welfare state"—represents an important part of the Big Deal struck to develop our human capital. Because all the pieces fit together, education can't be analyzed in isolation; nevertheless, most social spending transfers money among generations.

Almost 40 percent of our total federal budget goes to the elderly and their families through Social Security and Medicare.[16] About 30 percent of state and local spending goes to education.[17] In the year 2000, the United States provided public support for both children and the elderly—not counting medical expenditures—that came to about $10,000 per dependent per year.[18] A large proportion of the taxes that we pay represent either payback for our education or pay "forward" for our old age. The welfare state should really be dubbed the family state.

Both families and states try to manage their internal conflicts, and if they fail, they can fall apart. Both face pressures resulting from changes in our production of human capital. Children once became productive workers by about the age of twelve. Now, many of them do not hit the labor market until the age of twenty-two. Few elderly once reached that exalted state known as retirement. Now, most people expect to live twenty years or so after they have stopped working for pay. Not surprisingly, the taxes paid by the working-age population have increased in percentage terms.

As taxes go up, taxpayers look harder to see who is getting what, but current systems of accounting make it hard for them to tell. Tax rates are more visible than tax benefits, and progressive income taxes pinch the affluent in ways that mobilize them politically. Jostling for position should be expected in this game, but such jostling can be costly, especially without referees. And Americans often find it hard to decide what team they're really on.

GETTING WHAT YOU DESERVE

Everyone likes to invoke a version of the social contract, and educators are no exception. Many excellent reports on the decline of public higher education complain that our social contract has been broken.[19] They complain that we have not fulfilled our commitment to equality of opportunity, and I agree. That's why I think we need to think harder about how social contracts evolve. How did this commitment to public higher education emerge? Why has support for it diminished over the last twenty-five years? Better answers to these questions might help us remobilize support.

Every time I get on a plane and open one of the seat-pocket magazines, I see an ad that hasn't changed in twenty years: "In business, you don't get what you deserve; you get what you negotiate," explains a gray-haired but apparently ageless man named Chester Karass. Weirdly, long before these ads appeared, the novelist Kurt Vonnegut used the word *karass* to describe a group of people who voluntarily come together to get things done. In public education you don't get what you deserve, you get what your team can negotiate. Much depends on who is on your team, who it is allied with, and how much power it can wield. But much also depends on how well you can explain your ideas for a better deal.

2

THE SWEET BOOM

The best perks of teaching at a land-grant university are the relics of an earlier era, like the barns. On an early spring day, Buster the off-white pig lies in a mighty sleep. The sign on his pen asks visitors to refrain from feeding him treats, as he has been suffering from indigestion. This problem is currently under study by the students in charge. Meanwhile, they dote on a beautiful Morgan mare, Bay State Odyssey, who is big with foal, and after that they will tend the llama herd.

Okay, not many students will go into farming, and the polymer science and linguistics departments have a stronger national reputation. But the history of the institution matters, as does the larger history of higher education. Both illustrate the importance of the commons and the deals we've struck to govern it. Access to education helped Americans move toward their ideal of equal opportunity. Students learned more and earned more. Employers gained an educated, homegrown workforce. Taxpayers benefited especially in their old age. This part of the Big Deal generated a sweet boom in public higher education.

THE RISE OF STATE U

The school that eventually became UMass was carved out of the commons, an effort to transform land into a new factor of production: education. In 1862, shortly after the South seceded from the Union, Congress passed a bill that granted every state 30,000 acres of public land. Proceeds from the sale of this land endowed the study of agriculture and mechanical arts.

New Englanders were the strongest supporters. Their spokesman, Justin Morrill, after whom the new act was named, compared public support of education to the construction of lighthouses and harbors—boons to commerce. But he also described it as a ladder of opportunity. The so-called land-grant institutions that resulted from the Morrill Act opened the doors of higher education to women and blacks.[1]

Expanded opportunities reinforced the bootstrap vision of upward mobility that held the country together. The advice to "Go west, young man," combined with the practical opportunity of virtually free land offered by the Homestead Act, held men accountable for their own economic welfare. As land gradually became scarce and wage employment more common, education gained importance: "Go to school, young man, and crack the books." While increases in high school enrollment and graduation were a necessary first step, the possibility of attending college offered symbolic affirmation of an egalitarian ideal. Anyone, in principle, could become a gentleman.

The trajectory was easiest for white men. Still, the public commitment to higher education extended, in principle, to all. Justin Morrill stayed on task, and another legislative act in 1890 bearing his name established funding for dedicated— even if entirely segregated—colleges for African Americans in seventeen southern states. Americans spent more public money on higher education in the nineteenth century than did most European countries. We also implemented a less elitist system, in which students were less likely to be tracked at an early stage into vocational tasks. Geographic mobility seemed to contribute to intergenerational mobility as well. The U.S. economy as a whole got a boost, as Justin Morrill had promised that it would.[2]

Ardent faith in education rallied the advocates of the Progressive Era. John Dewey celebrated the "funded capital of civilization."[3] A new Boston Public Library, dubbed the "palace of the people," carved a strong message on its cornice: "The Commonwealth requires the education of the people as the safeguard of order and liberty." States and towns campaigned to increase high school attendance and graduation. Public higher education continued to expand, especially in the western states that lacked famous private colleges. Today's economic historians have dubbed the twentieth century the human capital century.[4]

IT WASN'T JUST DEMOCRACY

What drove this triumphal march? The economic payoff surely helped create a virtuous circle: technological change demanded literacy and problem-solving skills, which, in turn, boosted technological change. But not all countries followed this path, even though, presumably, they too had much to gain.

Democracy made a difference. Cross-national comparisons show that between 1880 and 1930, the higher the percentage of men who voted, the higher the levels of primary schooling.[5] The expansion of primary and then secondary education laid the foundation for the expansion of public universities.

Higher levels of democratic participation were also associated with the expansion of social spending, including public pensions. While one might assume that the majority felt empowered to impose its will upon—and thereby extract higher taxes from—the very rich, in fact primary and secondary schools were funded by local taxes and tended to receive more generous funding in communities where wealth was broadly distributed within a more homogeneous population.[6]

With the exception of the income tax levied to finance the Civil War, most other revenues came from taxes on imports, tobacco, and whiskey. These taxes might have weighed a bit more heavily on affluent than other families, but not by much.

Democracy's effects on education were complex and indirect, promoting a specific form of solidarity: social insurance. Pooling the costs of protection against risk could be quite efficient. Private insurance would always tend to exclude those most in need of it. Public insurance could solve that problem (though it could create other problems in its wake). Some early socialists described their vision as a vast insurance company for the bearing of all losses from fire, shipwreck, old age, and widowhood.[7] The promise of equal opportunity itself could be construed as insurance against the bad luck of being born into disadvantage.

Traditional family values had always emphasized the need

to balance rights with responsibilities, and solidarity based on kinship. Trade unionists called upon their brothers and sisters in the working class to unite and organize for change. The increased bargaining power of wage earners forced many of the concessions of the so-called welfare state. But the early welfare state itself increased solidarity by developing institutions—such as public education and public pensions—that linked the collective welfare of the generations.

Solidarity is almost always warmed by war. In the United States the first national pensions were awarded to soldiers wounded in the Revolutionary War, and to their widows and surviving dependents if they could show dire poverty. In an effort to help recruit soldiers for the Union Army, Congress promised similar pensions to all those wounded in the Civil War. By 1873, veterans' widows were allowed increased allowances based on their number of children. In 1890 pensions were extended to all those who had served and had subsequently become disabled, not just those who had been wounded. In 1906, military service in the Union Army became a sufficient condition to qualify for pensions. Many Southern states offered similar, though less generous, benefits to veterans of the Confederate Army.[8]

Early proponents of social insurance combined the pious rhetoric of family obligation with a populist critique of the disruptive impact of industrialization, urbanization, and immigration. Even though women lacked the right to vote, their civic participation in clubs and other groups amplified their political voice. Many states followed Illinois' lead in 1911, establishing Mothers' Pensions programs to provide support for widows and mothers abandoned by the fathers of their children.[9] These programs, often funded on the local rather than state level, varied considerably within individual states and provided only modest levels of support. Yet they represented a collective commitment to children's welfare.

Vulnerability at the other end of the life cycle also caused concerns. Less rooted in agricultural communities than they once were, living longer than ever before, and often receiving less support from their children, many elderly had become needy. Emboldened by the veterans' pensions precedent, groups like the Fraternal Order of the Eagles lobbied hard for old-age pensions, and, by 1935, thirty states had adopted them. Both the Mothers' and old-age pensions set the stage for the more ambitious federal Social Security Act passed in 1935.

The income tax that had funded the Union Army had been quite progressive. But it was eliminated as soon as the Civil War was won and paid for. Subsequent efforts to reestablish it met with judicial disapproval—overcome only by a Constitutional amendment in 1913, a banner victory of the Progressive Era. The Progressive Party Platform of 1912 confidently asserted principles of economic solidarity: "This country belongs to the people who inhabit it. Its resources, its business, its institutions and its laws should be utilized, maintained or altered in whatever manner will best promote the general interest. It is time to set the public welfare in the first place."[10] Public higher education would rely heavily on this vision of the commons.

MOMENTUM

Between 1900 and 1940, public higher education gained momentum, claiming a larger share of state and local spending, and steadily enrolling more students. The relative size of educational establishments increased, with a new emphasis on scientific research. Famous private universities such as Harvard retained their prestige, joined by relative newcomers established in the 1890s, including Stanford and the University of Chicago. But few new private universities were founded after 1900. Their market share declined. By 1940 almost 50 percent of college students were at public institutions, compared to only 22 percent in 1897.[11]

These were truly state-based institutions. In the Midwest and West, land-grant institutions tended to promote the research that would serve their local economies the best: the University of Wisconsin promoted dairy science; the University of Iowa promoted corn; the University of Colorado pursued mining technology. Taxpayers in a state were likely to capture the benefits of their investments. More than three-quarters of all students attended college in the same state in which they were born.[12]

State universities did not diminish enrollment at the private ones; rather, they pulled in students who would not otherwise have been able to afford a college education. In 1933, average tuition and fees at a public university came to $61—the equivalent of about $916 in 2005 dollars. By contrast, the average tuition and fees at a private institution in 1933 amounted to $265—the equivalent of $3,981 in 2005.[13] Patterns evident then persist today: states with higher levels of broadly distributed wealth (such as automobile ownership) invested more heavily in public higher education systems. However, states with many private colleges and universities (predominantly, but not exclusively, in New England) invested significantly less in their public systems.[14] Perhaps public investments seemed less necessary to them, since they already had universities in place. But tuition and fees remained higher at the privates; further, these institutions (particularly those with brand-name reputations) tended to attract more students from out-of-state who were also less likely to remain in-state after graduation.

In a sense, private institutions crowded out public investments. In states like Massachusetts, students from low-income families got less encouragement to attend college than in states like Iowa or Wisconsin. The likely mechanisms were political, reflecting team-based loyalties. Alumni of institutions like Harvard, Boston University, Boston College, Tufts, or Brandeis want to support their own schools and protect them from competition. They might prefer to make generous private donations and urge their own children to attend their alma maters, rather than pay taxes to educate other people's kids. (Ironically, the research summarized here detailing the early history of public higher education was conducted primarily by economists at Harvard.)

THE NEW DEAL AND THE GI BILL

After 1929, the U.S. economy fell into the Great Depression, increasing political pressure on the affluent to help buffer the effects of unemployment. Franklin D. Roosevelt's New Deal made explicit many of the features of the Big Deal described in chapter 1. Building on state-level precedents, the Social Security Act of 1935 formalized a new contractual arrangement for pooling the risks of unemployment, disability, old age, and loss of a family's primary wage earner.

Conservative policy makers would have preferred a self-financed system, with the federal government essentially banking contributions from the working-age population that they could draw upon later. Progressive policy makers would have preferred a universal system, with benefits unlinked from paid employment and work history. The actual legislation was forged by compromise: individuals would be required to make contributions, which would influence the level of benefits they would later receive. But the benefits that workers over the age of forty would later receive would far exceed the value of their contributions. The difference was made up by the contributions of younger workers, who could expect, in return, a later transfer from workers younger than themselves. As with most European pensions set up in the mid-twentieth century, pay-as-you-go seemed like the way to go.

World War II boosted national solidarity to new heights. The preceding years of economic depression, the growing visibility of the socialist economies, and the Roosevelt administration's New Deal set the stage. But the surprise attack at Pearl Harbor and the necessity of major economic mobilization to fight a war on two fronts intensified the political drama. The country taxed the rich to help pay for the war, establishing a top rate of 82 percent on taxable income that would be considered preposterous today. In partial compensation for the military draft, Congress passed the GI Bill, which offered every veteran complete reimbursement of tuition and a generous stipend to attend college.

The GI Bill enabled many veterans who would not otherwise have applied to college to sign up, symbolizing continued U.S. leadership in commitment to public higher education. (In contrast, Great Britain guaranteed its veterans public support only for the completion of secondary education.)[15] The bill also, at least temporarily, bridged the rift between public and private institutions described earlier, by providing what was essentially portable assistance. A veteran smart enough (and well-educated enough) to get into Harvard could get more support from the government than one who settled for UMass because the tuition paid by the GI Bill to Harvard was far higher. Still, many veterans landed in state universities, and taxpayers seemed eager to expand facilities to accommodate their needs.

The GI Bill strengthened the very sense of civic engagement and mutual obligation that had created it.[16] What had Americans fought for, if not to assert their confidence in democratic ideals? President Truman's Commission on Higher Education used language that, in retrospect, seems militant: "If college opportunities are restricted to those in the higher income brackets, the way is open to the creation and perpetuation of a class society which has no place in the American way of life."[17] The anxieties of the Cold War and the space race drove political commitments to improving university research.

TAXING AND SPENDING

The New Deal, combined with the "Good War," jolted the structure of public spending in the United States. Between 1930 and 1945, total federal, state, and local tax revenues jumped from about 10 percent of gross domestic product to about 25 percent. Then their percentage growth began to slow. Since 1970, total tax revenues have leveled off in percentage terms, averaging about 28 percent of GDP.[18] Despite much brouhaha and many changes in tax policy, a virtual cap seemed almost in effect, where decreased tax revenues in one area led to increases in another.

Social Security itself was the beneficiary of unexpected trends. Political pressures to expand eligibility and benefits were great, creating ever greater liabilities. While most low-wage workers (predominantly black and Hispanic) were initially excluded from coverage, a number of political factors—including the growing political mobilization of the elderly—led to their gradual inclusion.[19] Steady economic growth increased the tax revenues needed to meet those liabilities. The years between 1950 and 1974 were a kind of golden age for U.S. workers. Productivity gains translated into dramatic increases in real wages. That was truly an era of shared prosperity.[20]

An even happier trend for Social Security finance was the steady increase in married women's participation in paid employment. Most of these women were eligible, from the beginning, for pension benefits based on their husbands' earnings, even though married men were never asked to pay extra for these. As women started working outside the home, they started paying Social Security taxes on their own wages, but their benefits seldom increased. The new revenues made it feasible to fund Medicare for seniors in 1965 and to index Social Security payments against inflation in 1972. Pay-as-you-go was paying off.

THE CIVIL RIGHTS MOVEMENT AND FINANCIAL AID

Through the 1940s and early 1950s, education remained strictly segregated by race, most conspicuously in the South. In 1954, a Supreme Court decision outlawed explicit separation of the races in public schools, and the Civil Rights movement began gaining traction. The drama was often played out on college campuses. In 1962, an African American named James Meredith registered at the University of Mississippi. In the ensuing race riots, two people were killed. Meredith himself was pushed around, threatened, and ostracized by his fellow students as he went about the business of attending class.[21] But, a year later, Vivian Malone and James Hood stared down Governor George Wallace as he tried to block their entrance into the University of Alabama.[22]

Public outrage contributed to passage of the Civil Rights Act of 1964 and implementation of affirmative action policies. Overt discrimination on the basis of gender, race, or ethnicity was outlawed. The composition of the student body in colleges, universities, and professional training programs immediately began to shift. Young women from relatively well-to-do families that could afford to help them up the educational ladder were the most immediate beneficiaries. Both formal and informal restrictions on women's access to professional opportunities weakened, and their enrollment rates in business school, law school, and medical school began to climb. Even those who won their diplomas at the famous Seven Sister schools like Smith or Wellesley looked to graduate programs at the booming multiversities funded by the states.

The growing availability of financial aid urged all Americans on to college. Just as the Vietnam War began to expand, Lyndon Johnson threw his weight behind the Higher Education Act of 1965, which offered new funding for low-income students, including grants, work-study money, and government loans. The Education Amendments of 1972 developed a federal system of need-based assistance that students could use to attend either public or private schools. These came to be known as Pell Grants in honor of Claiborne Pell, U.S. senator from Rhode Island, who sponsored the legislation and also helped create the National Endowment for the Arts and the National Endowment for the Humanities.

The City University of New York (CUNY) represented, in many ways, the urban culmination of this trend, serving an extraordinarily diverse student body. Its member institutions provided especially important opportunities for Jewish intellectuals in the 1920s and 1930s when many Ivy League institutions discriminated against them. Consolidated under a new institutional umbrella in 1961, CUNY was free to city residents until 1975, when a municipal fiscal crisis led to the imposition of modest tuition rates. It has famously educated no fewer than twelve Nobel laureates.[23]

The California system, with its 1960 master plan, seemed to promise the most generous and democratic system of higher education imaginable.[24] And while the precursor of UMass, the Massachusetts Agricultural College, was better known for its prizewinning pumpkins than its scholars, state legislators recognized the need to expand opportunities for middle-class residents and middle-brow students with more classes for the masses, especially if they could be provided on the cheap. Economic development offered a partial rationale.

THE GOOD OLD DAYS

The first UMass alumni who won my heart started college in the 1940s. Izzy Rogoza, with fond memories of an economics professor who gave him a job chopping wood to help him stay in school (two bits an hour, if I remember correctly), endowed a lecture series. Sherry Barber, whose brothers were off fighting World War II, came to help out on her own terms. Economics degree in hand, she went to work for the War Board and later for the Women's Bureau. Regularly investing savings from her modest government salary, she accumulated a small fortune that she bequeathed to fund a lectureship in her mother's name. Tellingly, neither Izzy nor Sherry wanted to buy the right to put their names on a building.

Even the alums now in their fifties look back with nostalgia to the days when state universities were considered noble and grand. Funding was more generous then, and a degree from UMass was not so quickly and deplorably stamped with the non-Ivy brand. Public higher education helped fuel the very solidarity that drove it. Still, support for it was reinforced by payoffs to individuals and to U.S. society as a whole. As those payoffs began to shift, principles of equal opportunity would begin to seem more costly—too costly, it seems, for those who didn't need them.

> In 1815, Thomas Jefferson proposed "culling from every condition of our people the natural aristocracy of talents and virtue, and of preparing it by education, at the public expense, for the care of public concerns." [25]

> President Lyndon B. Johnson explained the vision behind the 1965 Higher Education Act as follows: "A high school student anywhere in this great land of ours can apply to any college or any university in any of the fifty states and not be turned away because his family is poor." [26]

3

THE SLOW FIZZLE

The 1970s were the golden age of public higher education. The American Dream Machine seemed full of gas and some of us thought we could drive it to utopia. But in the 1980s, the engine began to stutter, and it soon became apparent that it wasn't getting the necessary fuel. It was as though someone had poured water in the tank. The widespread political support that many of us had taken for granted began to be gradually, unevenly, but relentlessly withdrawn. It wasn't just the money. It was the spirit of the day. A backlash against public higher education was underway, part of a larger backlash against public anything and everything. Parts of the Big Deal were coming undone. Only recently has it begun to seem possible that we could put it back together on better terms.

State appropriations for universities all across the country began to zigzag and sag. Tuition and fees were jacked up to compensate. Financial aid did not keep pace, and much of it was redirected from low-income students to academic superstars. In 2005, state and local funding per student at public colleges and universities, adjusted for inflation, was at its lowest level in twenty-five years.[1] The titles of reports and headlines of newspaper stories told the story pretty well: "Broken Promises," "Slamming Shut the Doors," "Left Behind," "Scandals of Higher Education," "Bastions of Privilege," and "Engines of Inequality."[2] Withdrawal of support for state universities went along with tax cuts for the rich and a major assault on Social Security. It was part of what Paul Krugman calls "The Great Divergence"—a period of increased income inequality in which the top 1 percent of the population captured most of the real gains from economic growth.[3]

PULLING THE PLUG

The battery of standardized exams students take when they apply to college should begin with the following question: When does a state university stop being a state university? Multiple choices, and more than one answer may be correct. But rub the lead of your number two pencil into the little bubble in front of this one: when the state stops supporting it. The percentage of total spending at state universities provided by state tax revenues has been sinking for more than twenty years. Less than a third of the total budget of state universities today actually comes out of state tax revenues. As Jim Duderstadt, former president of the University of Michigan, put it, "We used to be state-supported, then state-assisted, and now we are state-located."[4]

This is the proximate reason for jumps in the sticker price of state universities. My file of clippings on the subject dates back to a time long before a Googling of it would yield ten thousand hits. Back in 1992, *BusinessWeek* noted "A Lot Less Moola Moola on Campus."[5] Students and their families paid 24 percent of the total costs in the early 1980s; by 2008, their share had risen to more than 36 percent.[6] In fiscal year 2007,

Massachusetts state appropriations represented only about 27 percent of the budget for the flagship Amherst campus.[7] Even this modest percentage leaves the campus vulnerable to a sudden cutback. Facing this fear, many state universities have chosen to "self-privatize." At the University of Virginia and the University of Colorado, state revenues cover less than 10 percent of the budget.[8]

For the last twenty-five years, the price of a college education has gone up faster than just about everything else except health care. In the United States, since 1980 the average cost of tuition and fees has far outstripped the supply of financial aid, much of which is targeted to students who may need it least.[9] While public colleges and universities are still far cheaper than privates ones, their price increases have been relentless—4.5 percent per year over and above the rate of inflation between the academic years 1998–99 and 2008–2009.[10]

As a result of financial aid, the actual cost of attending both public and private institutions is considerably below the sticker price. About two-thirds of students got some kind of financial aid in 2007–2008, and the average amount was $9,100.[11] Combined with the impact of new federal tax breaks (the Hope Scholarship, Lifelong Learning Credit, and new deductibility for college expenses), these subsidies almost counterbalanced the increase in average tuition and fees for middle-income families.

But the students who need aid most were not the ones who got it. A declining proportion of all federal, state, and institutional aid has been based on financial need. Increased federal spending on the Pell Grant program did not keep pace with the number of students qualifying for assistance, leading to declines in the average level of the award. In 1979–1980, the maximum grant covered about 77 percent of the average price of tuition, fees, and on-campus room and board at a public four-year institution; by 2007 it covered only 36 percent.[12] As a result, students became far more dependent on loans, and their debt burden grew steadily heavier.

Among the many tireless advocates trying to publicize this issue, the National Center for Public Policy and Higher Education deserves special credit for finding a catchy way to frame it. Their regular report, entitled *Measuring Up*, grades states on several indicators of performance, including college affordability. The number of states with a failing grade went from three in 2000 to thirteen in 2002, thirty-six in 2004, and forty-three in 2006.[13] Their 2008 report gave every state except California (which got a C-) an F.[14] Then, in 2009, the California state budget pretty much fell apart.

DOWN WITH THE PUBLIC

Asked to explain this trend, many people say something like "Taxes were going up and up, and at some point it just had to stop." But overall, taxes *weren't* going up and up between 1980 and 2000. As pointed out in the preceding chapter, they were stuck at about 28 percent of gross domestic product, where they had been for decades.[15] And its not as though these taxes were disappearing into a black hole. They were paying for valuable benefits, including education, health care, and income security in old age. But it is easier for individuals to see the costs than the benefits. Few have a clear picture of their net taxes—the difference between what they pay in and what they take out.

Net taxes are much harder to figure out than those numbers on your W2 form. Even experts in public finance are befuddled by them. The increasing complexity of both personal and public budgets contributed to accumulating aggravation with government spending in the 1970s, forming a strange meteorology of psychology and economics—a kind of perfect storm. Some deep underlying conflicts that nobody really wanted to talk about generated a stream of negatively charged electrons, and tax revolt became the lightening rod (discussed in more detail in chapter 7).

Growing inequality of wealth and income propelled powerful individuals into the top tax brackets, sparking a major political effort to reduce income taxes on the rich. Ronald Reagan led the way, but Democrats as well as Republicans jumped on board. In 1986, a major tax reform lowered the top income tax rate (paid primarily by those at the highest end) from 50 percent to 28 percent while increasing the lowest rate (paid primarily by those at the bottom end) from 11 percent to 15 percent. During the Clinton administrations, from 1993–2001, the top income rate was ratcheted back up slightly (to 38.6 percent), and the Earned Income Tax Credit provided new relief to low-income families.

George W. Bush's promise to resume tax cuts helped get him elected in 2000. With the help of a Republican Congress, he delivered the goods: cuts in the capital gains tax and estate taxes, as well as a decline in the top income tax rate, offered huge benefits to the roughly 3 percent of all U.S. families with incomes over $200,000 per year. The resulting loss of revenue led to huge increases in both federal and state budget deficits.[16] Once the party of fiscal responsibility, Republicans began to argue that large deficits were good because they would discourage further spending. In the immortal words of Grover Norquist, president of the antitax lobbying group Americans for Tax Reform, the Republican goal was not to abolish government but to reduce it to the size where it could be dragged into the bathroom and drowned in the bathtub. All the rubber duckies seemed to be lining up until Hurricane Katrina struck in 2005. The televised neglect of New Orleans' most vulnerable residents shocked most of those who viewed it. How could this happen in the richest nation in the world?

Growing anger and frustration with the war in Iraq also began to undermine Republican arguments that the nation could not afford to increase social spending. Over $915 billion public dollars were allocated to wars in Iraq and Afghanistan through the end of fiscal year 2009. The National Priorities Project calculates that this money could have paid for 140 million one-year scholarships to public universities.[17] Burgeoning expenditures on prisons became another conspicuous example of misplaced spending priorities. Mandatory sentencing and harsh punishments for small drug-related offenses increased spending on incarceration throughout the 1990s. The per-person costs of prison now exceed tuition at Harvard University. States can be benchmarked by the point in their budgetary history at which spending on incarceration began to exceed spending on their university systems. California reached this point in 1995, Massachusetts in 2003, Oregon in 2007.[18]

Growing inequality seemed to feed upon itself. The greater the distance between the rich and everybody else, the less the rich seemed to care about the rest of us. Throughout the 1980s and 1990s, economic and cultural segregation intensified, fueling a kind of opt-out strategy. Public schools bad? Send your children to private ones. Neighborhood going downhill? Buy into a gated community. Local beaches polluted? Fly to Bermuda for a vacation. Worried about retirement? Put more into your 401–3B and regular and Roth IRAs. State university losing quality? Quick, get your kids into a liberal arts college, preferably one with a high ranking in *U.S. News and World Report*.

The rhetoric of economic self-interest became so powerful that departures from it began to seem poetic. The most poignant testimony against repeal of the estate tax came from those who stood to gain the most. In a report titled "I Didn't Do It Alone" published by Responsible Wealth, several gazillionaires, including Warren Buffett, acknowledged that public support—including that of state universities—explained a large part of their personal success.[19] These were traitors in what the *Wall Street Journal* came to call a "class war" over taxes.[20] But the persistent growing power of the antitax army may owe less to its loyalists (and control of many media sources) than to changes in the global economy.

FOOTLOOSE BUT NOT FANCY FREE

Both individual students and individual businesses are less rooted in their local communities than they once were. For most of the twentieth century, individuals born in a state were likely to attend college and become taxpayers in the same state. Gradually, however, a national market for education developed. Between 1949 and 1994, the percentage of students who attended college in their own states fell from about 93 percent to about 75 percent.[21] Parents—particularly the relatively high-income parents likely to be able to send their children to college out of state—had less economic incentive to support public higher education.

Many high-paying professional jobs are part of a national, rather than a local, market. Increased mobility after college means that individual states are less likely to capture the gains from investing in their own students. Highly educated workers remain a boon for cities seeking investment—but these cities don't have to grow their own, just attract them. An estimated 56 percent of UMass Amherst graduates remain in the state after graduation—surely higher than the percentage of graduates from Harvard or MIT, but still low enough to make state taxpayers wonder.[22] Because of their land-grant legacy, many state universities are located in small towns in relatively rural areas. These communities get a direct boost from the education industry but seldom wield much political influence on the state level.

Research and development at state universities still offers big economic payoffs. But these payoffs, now less linked to agriculture, are also less state-specific than they once were. The University of Wisconsin no longer prioritizes the dairy industry, and UMass is better known for polymer than cranberry-cultivation science. Many graduate students, especially in the sciences, come not just from out of state but from out of country. The percentage of science and engineering doctorates awarded to foreign-born students increased from 23 percent in 1966 to 39 percent in 2000.[23]

Many of these scientists produce benefits for the entire world, and, because most remain in this country after graduation, they boost the U.S. economy as a whole. But ordinary taxpayers in Wisconsin or Massachusetts may wonder why they should foot the bill. And while many of these taxpayers might agree, in principle, that academic competition should be completely performance-based, they may be aggrieved when their daughter or son can't get public funding for graduate school. Talented foreign students with access to good universities in their own countries represent formidable competitors for U.S.-born college graduates, especially in the sciences.[24]

Applications for the graduate program in economics at UMass Amherst from students in India, China, the former Soviet Union, and Turkey outnumber applications from U.S.-born students by a factor of about three to one. These students have achieved extremely high test scores, not only on the Graduate Record Exams (GRE) but also on the Test of English as a Foreign Language (TOEFL). If we admitted students based on test score rankings alone, few if any U.S. students would make the final cut. Though few graduate admissions committees would admit the truth, most apply an informal quota system, a kind of affirmative action for U.S. citizens.

Increased corporate mobility has also cut into state tax coffers. Footloose industries who threaten to relocate can extract major tax concessions from states and local communities. Such threats, combined with other aggressive tax minimization strategies, have reduced the contribution that corporate taxes once made to state tax revenues.[25] While the technical term for this is "intensification of interjurisdictional tax competition," two economists at the Federal Reserve Bank of Minnesota came up with a better term: the War Among the States.[26] Declining corporate income tax rates have increased the burden of taxes on ordinary people. State taxes tend to be regressive—especially in states without a progressive income tax.[27] As a result, low- and middle-income families often bear the brunt of state efforts to increase funding for education at every level.

These same families are most vulnerable to job loss, easily held hostage by corporate threats to downsize or outsource good jobs. The Massachusetts melodrama has been particularly intense. In 1995, both Raytheon and Fidelity Investments threatened to move jobs out of state unless they received major tax concessions. Governor William Weld urged the legislature to cooperate, explaining, "If you think the textile industry moved south in a hurry over the weekend in the 1950s, watch what can happen in other industries."[28] *Boston Globe* cartoonist Dan Wasserman put a sharper edge on it with a cartoon showing a Raytheon operative in a trench coat making a call from a phone booth: "Listen up, Massachusetts, deliver $40 million in a paper bag or you'll never see your jobs again."

Whether the threats were real or not, they were backed by an intensive lobbying campaign that recruited both Democrats and Republicans and inaccurately claimed that Massachusetts tax rates were among the highest in the nation. The legislature gave in to the pressure but failed to obtain any long-run guarantees in return. Raytheon continued to downsize, and Fidelity escalated its outsourcing of front-office financial jobs overseas.

Such tax breaks have relatively little effect because virtually every state is offering them.[29] In fiscal 2004, the estimated value of corporate tax breaks designed to promote economic development in Massachusetts was about $800 million, more than the total amount then-governor Mitt Romney proposed for total spending on higher education in the state.[30]

Even more consequential was a larger campaign to cut all taxes. Between 1996 and 2002, a combination of cuts in personal income, capital gains, corporate, and sales taxes sacrificed about $5.5 billion in revenue.[31] State policy makers, primed by reports from conservative think tanks, blamed fiscal woes on the stock market crash of 2001 and moaned about the ups and downs of the business cycle. But by fiscal year 2004, the ratio of all taxes, fees, and charges levied by the Commonwealth on personal income in the state was lower than that in forty-two other states. In the same year, Massachusetts ranked fiftieth in spending on higher education as a percentage of income.[32]

LIKE NATION, LIKE STATE

Many U.S. states, including California and New York, have economies and populations bigger than some countries. Thus competition among states for business is also carrying over to the global level, with less immediate but, in the long run, more momentous consequences. While globalization offers some terrific benefits, it imposes some terrifying risks. Many of us (in general, the college-educated) are gaining greater access to private goods. But all of us are losing the incentive—and perhaps even the potential—to cooperate in the provision of public goods. Like our global climate and water supply, human and social capabilities are assets that cannot be privately owned. Their creation, development, and maintenance require collaboration.

Because we don't measure the value of these public goods, they get less attention than the private goods and services measured in our gross domestic product. Free trade and increased mobility of investment across the globe deliver visible and impressive benefits. The demonstrable gains might be big enough to compensate for small "externalities," "negative spillovers," or the unfair losses that some vulnerable groups (like those, worldwide, without a college degree) might experience, but there is no evidence that these gains are actually being redistributed from winners to losers. We have pretty good tools for analyzing the plus side of the ledger—the new technologies, the new assets, the new flows—but we don't know how to measure the cost side of the ledger. What is our rate of environmental depreciation? What is the threat of endemic terrorism and devastating global war? What is the cost of downward mobility and increased inequality?

As most people have now figured out, American workers without a college degree (and many with) have been hammered by increased international competition and decreased demand for their labor. The typical high school graduate earned less in 2007 than in 1973—about $15.00 an hour, adjusted for inflation.[33] They weren't getting much more in terms of benefits, either; access to health and pension benefits declined, especially at the bottom of the labor market.[34] Few college professors have wrung their hands over this trend. If anything, they have used the numbers to try to persuade their students to work harder for their diplomas.

Now, workers with college degrees and advanced professional training are also facing a gloomy future, and economists are paying more attention. In 2004, Nobel prize winner Paul Samuelson publicly chided his colleagues for assuming that increased competition from highly skilled workers in Asia would necessarily benefit U.S. workers, emphasizing the ways that our trading partners are increasing their own comparative advantage in producing college-educated workers.[35] As Princeton economist Alan Blinder elaborates, a country's comparative advantage in international trade is no longer a function of climate or geography—but rather is often the result of human effort.[36] He might have added "collective human effort," as in the establishment of top-rate highly subsidized public education.

The United States no longer provides the majority of the world's highly educated labor: in the early 1970s, we produced about 50 percent of all the world's doctorates; by 2010 our projected share will be 15 percent.[37] Several European countries, as well as South Korea, now send a larger proportion of their youth to college than we do. Increases in the global supply of skilled labor have created a new terminology: "human resource leapfrogging."

Thomas Friedman, sounding as upbeat as possible about this trend in his bestseller *The World Is Flat*, advises his own daughters: "Girls, finish your homework—people in China and India are starving for your jobs." [38] But Friedman naively assumes that the United States is one big team, like the U.S. Olympic basketball team in 1994 (which in his opinion just didn't try hard enough to win). [39] Hello, Tom! Corporate CEOs don't represent the United States. According to economist Milton Friedman, their only responsibility is to make as much money for their shareholders as possible. [40]

The ability of high-tech firms to import highly trained workers from overseas through the H1-B visa program has long reduced the demand for U.S.-trained computer and software engineers. Norm Matloff, one of the few outspoken critics of this policy, began publicizing data demonstrating this point in 1998. [41] Matloff also emphasized that programmers entering the country under H1-B visas must apply for permission to change jobs and require company sponsorship in order to obtain permanent residence. As a result, they are easily held hostage by employers who can pay them less and work them harder than U.S. citizens. For years Matloff was treated like a xenophobic kook.

By 2006, however, the flames of backlash against immigration began to singe even those at the highest levels. A member of the Programmer's Guild discovered a Pittsburgh law firm's video explaining how to finesse the requirement that firms sponsoring an H1-B employee for permanent residency demonstrate that no U.S. worker is qualified. Deftly edited and posted on YouTube, the video clip showed just how opportunistic employers can be in their efforts to reduce their labor costs. The cinematic evidence rendered even a Republican congressman from Texas apoplectic. [42]

In another poignant example of digital resistance, a disgruntled IBM worker in 2003 distributed a recording of a conference call in which the corporation's top employee relations executives explained the need to move high-paying white-collar jobs overseas even though that might create a "backlash." One high technology consulting group estimates that as many 450,000 computer-industry jobs could be transferred abroad in the next twelve years—about 8 percent of the total.[43]

Just as Raytheon sees little private benefit in investing in the University of Massachusetts, multinational corporations see little private benefit in investing in public higher education in the United States as a whole. These businesses are no longer dependent on workers in their own countries. Why grow your own if someone else can do it more cheaply? The services of parents, as well as of teachers, are cheaper overseas. Corporate interests and national interests have never been perfectly aligned. Their current divergence, however, is driving a process of political realignment and creating new openings for change.

RECONFIGURATION

The Big Deal has always been a bit unstable, more so now that the economic boundaries of the nation-state are paper thin. The changes described in this chapter strengthened the political power of groups with little stake in the well-being of ordinary Americans. Yet the success of efforts to cut both taxes and social spending rested heavily on the claim that ordinary Americans would benefit. The Great Recession starting in 2008 made it very clear that they have not. The negative impact of reduced commitment to both education and a social safety net has become too conspicuous to hide.

Global economic competition—as well as the growing threat of global environmental problems—will inevitably make it harder for Americans to enjoy rapid economic growth. But that is exactly why Americans could rally around the challenge to develop more cooperative, sustainable, and egalitarian economic policies. Public support for public education remains strong, as does public support for payback to the elderly for their investment in the young. Periodically, the limits of a system based on nothing but the pursuit of individual self-interest become particularly apparent, backlit by problems like global war and global warming that can't be solved without better, smarter forms of cooperation. As a bumper sticker puts it, "If you think education is expensive, try ignorance."

"My view is that the policy choices that we made between 1862 (the first Morrill Act) and about 1980 were consistently progressive, expansionary, and inclusive. Since about 1980 our federal, state, and four-year institutional policy choices have been consistently regressive, constrictive, and exclusive." —Tom Mortenson[44]

In 2003, the flagship universities, along with a group of other public research universities just like them, spent $257 million on financial aid for students from families that earn more than $100,000 per year—considerably more than the $171 million they spent on families at the other end of the economic spectrum who earned less than $20,000 per year.[45]

4

STICKER SHOCKS

Lanky young guy, baseball hat on backwards, carrying standard-issue backpack, doesn't say much in class but does his homework and writes a surprisingly good first paper. I'm puzzled when his name still hasn't appeared on my roster by the sixth week and he has disappeared. A month later I run into him at Starbucks, where he pulls me a tall skinny latte. "Hey, what happened to you?" I ask. "Hey," he answers, with a rueful smile, "the check bounced." I understand that he means the check to the university registrar. Who was that bad check from? His parents? Himself? Or the rest of us?

The price of higher education is not simply going up. It's going up in a confusing, unpredictable, and aggravating way, like the cost of private health insurance. Middle-income families rush to buy the magazine with the latest college rankings out of a desperate determination to get the best of deals. Low-income families look the other way because they're pretty sure they can't afford to buy. Many students decide that they don't want to play an expensive game that will make them feel like losers even if, in the end, they would be better off.

That old adage "It takes money to make money" has morphed into a cruel new form. In the United States today, students need an education to get an education, in more ways than one. College-educated parents know how to stay on task: Buy a house in a good school district, no matter what it costs. Encourage good grades through strategic deployment of carrots, sticks, soccer games, and ballet lessons. Take them on the college tour, and then you can start writing the bigger checks. Not to say that college-educated parents have it easy, or that first-generation college students can't ever make it on their own. But that neon advertisement of equal opportunity blinks on and off enough to make you wonder if you're seeing straight.

PANIC ATTACKS

Let's start with the good news for a change. More students are enrolling in college than ever before, and even if they have to borrow money to pay their bills at a state university, the average debt is not that much greater than that for a new car. College can be fun, and not just because the parties start on Thursday night. Many students like learning new things, meeting new people, growing into themselves. They gain capabilities that can help them change the world as well as earn a bigger paycheck.

The College Board, the nonprofit organization that develops and administers standardized tests for potential college students, does its best to reassure. The splash page of its Web site exhorts its readers to be brave:

For example, did you know that about 56 percent of students attend four-year schools with annual tuition and fees below $9,000? After grants are taken into consideration, the net price the average undergraduate pays for a college education is significantly lower than the published tuition and fees. And remember, other forms of financial aid will further reduce the amount your family will actually pay.[1]

Why so much panic and frustration, then? For one thing, students have little control over what state they live in, a factor which greatly affects the costs to them of attending a public school. For another, prices keep rising.[2]

Even those planning on attending a private school see the publics as a fallback. For many parents and students, the cost of attending a public state university represents the bottom end, the minimum investment, the lowball estimate of what it will cost to launch their children into successful self-sufficiency. Evolution has selected primates for their ability to adapt to changes in the environment that threaten their offspring. When they don't understand those changes, they start rattling the bars, making their indignation known.

Tuition and fees at UMass Amherst represent the cutting edge of the general trends described in the preceding chapter. Figure 1 shows the tidal waves trending upward through peaks and troughs. In-state tuition alone is not much higher than it was 1977, because the state legislature forbade tuition increases—a bit like ordering the ocean not to rise. In order to pay its bills in the absence of public support, the university had to raise its out-of-state fees, and that increase drove the trend.

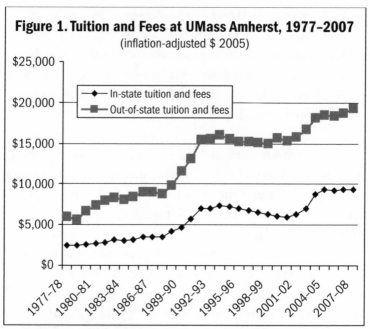

Figure 1. Tuition and Fees at UMass Amherst, 1977–2007
(inflation-adjusted $ 2005)

Source: University of Massachusetts Amherst, Office of Academic Planning and Assessment

Consider the picture from the point of view of an out-of-state student who enrolled in 2004—perhaps choosing a public university over a private one because it was cheaper even when taking competing financial aid packages into account. But, oops, just as she figured out how the place works and learned to like it, the price got hiked. Out-of-state students are considered less sensitive to price increases (if they couldn't afford out-of-state tuition, they would be going in-state). They are the cash cows that help finance the in-states, providing an incentive to recruit more of them.

A lot of students just choose not to think about affordability issues because such issues are so . . . unpleasant. But some grasp the nettle firmly and protest. A student-organized hearing at UMass Amherst in December 2007 called witnesses to testify. Lindsay McCulkan, a well-spoken activist with PHE-NOM (Public Higher Education Network of Massachusetts), provided an overview: between 2001 and 2004, UMass Amherst cut aid by 33 percent. In inflation-adjusted dollars, she explained, total financial aid was lower than in 1988.[3]

A shy junior named Ila took the stand: "I'm speaking for myself but also for the missing—those who have to work, those who never made it here. My parents couldn't afford to help me out very much. That's my testimony." The next witness, Shannon Copley, was angry. "I'm here against the odds," she said. "I'm from Hartford—a city where everyone who can afford to move out and live in the suburbs does. The financial aid forms said that our expected family contribution to college expenses was zero—that's how low our income is. But by the time I graduate we (my family and I) will be $40,000 in debt." She added, "I came here because I wanted to make my community a better place, but now I don't see how I can."

PARENTAL POCKETBOOKS

The textbooks that I am supposed to teach from explain that young adults invest in their own human capital by deciding to attend college. We are supposed to be smart investors as well as happy consumers, even if we haven't any money in the bank. In the real world, students themselves pay for only about a quarter of their college costs. On average, public subsidies and public and private financial aid pay about half the costs, and parents pay another 25 percent.[4] So parents are, on average, splitting half the costs with the kids. (Keep in mind that kids are not, in general, splitting the benefits.) And no matter how much parents love their kids, they still have to pay their own bills for health insurance and retirement.

Did they really know what they were getting into? Children are bundles of joy, but they are also an important crop, and appropriately enough, the Department of Agriculture issues regular estimates of what parents spend on them up through age seventeen—excluding the cost of college. By their calculation, a middle-income, husband-wife family with two children in 2000 could expect to spend about $165,630 per child over eighteen years.[5] This estimate completely omits the value of the time that parents devote to direct and indirect care of their children (which more than doubles the dollar cost).[6] It also omits the value of parental contributions to the cost of four years of college, which increase the cash expenditures estimate by about 10 percent, and even more for students who attend selective private schools.[7]

If you were as profit-oriented as the *Wall Street Journal* thinks you should be, you would never raise children. If you reallocated hypothetical expenditures on two offspring to investments enjoying an average 5 percent annual rate of return, you could retire with a nest egg of more than $2 million. All else being equal, you would be much better off than the individuals who raise new little units of human capital and send them to college so they can earn higher wages and pay the Social Security taxes that help finance the retirement of people who never raised kids.

No wonder an article in the *Wall Street Journal* asks, "Is it so wrong to expect your kids to pay for at least some of their own college education?"[8] Parents have no legal obligation to contribute, but if they refuse, other sources of aid are restricted. The presumption of parental responsibility is built into federal student aid procedures, which require filing of standard financial need statements.[9] Financial aid is based on parental "ability to pay," not "willingness to pay." If parents refuse to provide the amount that the guidelines stipulate, their kids run into serious trouble. They get no dispensation unless they are willing to forgo college long enough to establish their economic independence. One online guide to financial aid devotes an entire section to the question "What can you do if your parents refuse to help?"[10]

Most college-educated parents want to send their own children to college in return for what their parents did for them. Many low-income parents would like to do the same. But those who never received gifts find it more difficult to give them. Most non-college-educated parents have seen their real earnings stagnate or decline even as their own health insurance and pension costs have increased. Add to this the fact that parents and children often disagree on educational goals, and that a history of family conflict generally reduces the probability of support. Children of divorced parents are less likely to enjoy help than those from intact families.[11]

ALPHABET CITY
Even if parents are willing and undaunted by the declining level of need-based aid, they face an application gauntlet. The

paperwork is harder, and more time-consuming, than filing income taxes. The Obama administration has recently implemented some major improvements, but radical simplification apparently requires congressional action.[12]

In order to calculate their expected family contribution (EFC), parents have to fill out the FAFSA (Free Application for Federal Student Aid) and/or the CSS (College Scholarship Service) profile for the slightly different aid formula used by a large number of schools for their own aid disbursement. Then there is the PLUS (Parent Loan for Undergraduate Student) loan and possible eligibility for a SEOG (Supplemental Educational Opportunity Grant). Fortunately, as a result of the GPRA (Government Performance and Results Act) of 1993, the GAO (General Accounting Office) officially reported that this complexity had gotten out of hand.[13]

Professionals have stepped into the market niche, with college financial planning services that enable parents to legally and ethically minimize their EFC and maximize their aid. These pros will not only complete your FAFSA, they will compose a letter to the university financial aid office and negotiate with the school on your behalf. If you can afford to pay them, along with the accountants required to file your income tax and negotiate with your health insurance provider, you'll be sitting pretty. Meanwhile, if you'd like to know who actually gets most of the benefits of our baroque financial aid system, you will need to hire an economist to conduct a detailed analysis of the NPSAS (National Postsecondary Student Aid Survey).

If you assume that students behave like trained MBAs,

confidently assessing costs and benefits, such details will appear unimportant. If you accept the possibility that applicants are likely to be daunted and discouraged by complexity, the paperwork problems become more salient. They could go a long way toward explaining why financial aid often fails to reach those who need it most.[14]

The official "expected family contribution" is based on a progressive formula that resembles our current federal income tax system. Because higher-income families must pay more, they are essentially "taxed" at a higher rate.[15] But like the federal income tax system, the financial aid system has loopholes big enough to drive a brand new Prius through. The income and assets of grandparents or other family members are not taken into account. Financial advisors routinely advise grandparents to avoid adding gifts to a college savings account in which it would be counted.[16] In a recent survey of families saving for college, about one-third said they expected financial assistance from grandparents and other relatives.[17]

The bottom line is that low-income students are even less likely than others to compare the real costs of college (net of financial aid) against the possible benefits. Their decision to buy is strongly influenced by actual tuition and fees, the "sticker price."[18] That's one reason why most of those who go to college end up in public, rather than in private, schools.

SHOPPING 101

When the going gets tough, the tough go shopping. But some things are harder to buy than others. Admission to a specific college is not a commodity whose qualities can be easily assessed up front. It's a ticket to a complex set of services that you must combine with your own effort and initiative. It will allow you to choose a ladder into a shifting hierarchy of occupations, but you won't know until you have climbed a long time whether it is taking you where you really want to go. The decision to attend a specific college or university will change who you hang out with and who you are.

Table 1. The Priciest Privates and Cheapest Publics, 2006–2007

		Tuition, Fees, Room and Board (in-state for public schools)
	Most Expensive Private Schools:	
1.	Sarah Lawrence College	$48,240
2.	George Washington University	$46,730
3.	Georgetown University	$45,320
4.	New York University	$45,200
5.	Boston College	$45,944
	Least Expensive Public Schools:	
1.	Tennessee State University	$2,390
2.	San Diego State University	$3,122
3.	University of Florida	$3,206
4.	Florida A&M University	$3,269
5.	Florida State University	$3,307

Source: *U.S. News and World Report, Ultimate College Guide, 2008* (Naperville, IL 2008), pp. 136, 144.

The variation in what students and their families pay per year is stunning. The annual *U.S. News and World Report, Ultimate College Guide* offers a section on the "priciest privates," followed up by a section on the "cheapest publics." [19] In 2006–2007 one could pay $48,240 to attend Sarah Lawrence, or $2,390 (for residents) to attend Tennessee State (see Table 1). If you want to attend a public university, it's best to decide in advance what state you want your family to live in. UMass Amherst is one of the more expensive schools for in-state students, at $9,595. Still, it's considerably cheaper than the University of Vermont ($12,138) or Wayne State in Michigan ($13,925).

Table 2. Where America Went to College in 2003

	Community Colleges	Public Four-Year Colleges	Private Colleges	For-Profit Colleges
Number of Institutions	1,101	612	1,676	808
Undergraduate Enrollment	5.7 million	4.8 million	2.2 million	403,000
Average Tuition	$1,735	$4,081	$18,273	$11,043
Amount Spent to Educate a Student	$5,000–$9,000	$7,000–$25,000	$12,000–$80,000	$8,000–$10,000
Share of Entering Freshmen Who Earn BAs after 5 Years	7%*	47%	62%	1%**

*Refers to those who go on to four-year schools.

**In this time, 57 percent earn an associate's degree.

Source: *Business Week*, April 28, 2003, available at http:www.businessweek.com/magazine/content/03_17/b3830014.htm (accessed July 4, 2009).

The variation in what students get for the money is harder to pin down. Expenditures per student provide one indicator, but even these are hard to summarize. *BusinessWeek* made a valiant effort in 2003 (see Table 2). Spending per student at community colleges was modest, less than $10,000 per year.

At public four-year colleges, the next largest category, expenditures per student were higher, ranging from about $7,000 to about $25,000 per year. Private colleges registered the highest variation, from $12,000 to $80,000 per student. The for-profit colleges (more on these in chapter 6) are competing mostly with community colleges, spending about the same per student.

Both the community colleges and the for-profits tend to enroll students who are less committed to getting a diploma, so it's not surprising that the share of entering students who earn BAs within five years is very low (see Table 2, bottom row). What's shocking is that less than 50 percent of students entering four-year public school, on average, get their diplomas at that school. Average completion rates are higher in privates than in publics, at 62 percent, partly reflecting selection effects—students whose families are willing to pay more are likely to try harder. It's also possible that high costs serve as a kind of commitment device. Sinking more money into something can increase your determination to see it through.

Estimates of graduation rates are biased downward by the failure to track students who transfer to other institutions. Still, they show that admission to college is a risky purchase. No matter how much money you spend on it, it may not work. It's not that the product itself is faulty, as with some expensive coffee grinder that just falls apart. It's that the product is complex and unpredictable. Its success depends largely on the consumer's motivation. Its most important promise, therefore, lies in its potential to enhance that motivation.

BUYING THE BEST

This helps explain why many families want to send their children to a private school, even though it costs about four times as much, on average, as a public school.[20] The "selectives," including but not limited to the Ivy League, are especially attractive. The facilities can be awe-inspiring—some combination of country club and cathedral. The faculty can be the best that money can buy. If these two factors combine to allow a school to reject a large proportion of their applicants, their selectivity itself becomes a plus. Those who enroll are promised the best possible "peer effects": surrounded by excellence, they hope to become more excellent themselves.[21] Prestige itself is motivational.

The selective privates spend far more per student than the publics. They offer better facilities and probably, on average, better faculty. The differences between these two spheres of higher education have been steadily widening over time.[22] In 1980–1981, the average salary earned by full professors at Ph.D.-granting public universities amounted to 91 percent of the average for their counterparts at private universities. But the pay penalty for teaching at a public college or university has grown steadily over time. In 2006–2007, people like me earned 76 percent of what they would at a private institution.[23]

Few public universities can match the selectives for the simple reason that they don't have as much money to spend. Here's the technical explanation offered by economist Caroline Hoxby: "Because they are constrained, public colleges are generally unable to compete in the upper region of quality space."[24] A *BusinessWeek* writer refers more poetically to the "gilding of the Ivies."[25] Gilding would do no harm if the rest of us were left untarnished. Instead, we've seen the unpredictability of state funding drive administrators to distraction (and into the private sector) and leave us in drafty buildings with leaky roofs.

Not surprisingly, the relative quality of faculty at the publics has also declined. At UMass Amherst in 1994–1995, tenure track faculty taught 69 percent of all students, but by 2002–2003, the percentage was only 59 percent.[26] National statistics show a rapid increase in reliance on part-timers, who represented 22 percent of all faculty in 1970 but more than double that, 48 percent, in 2005.[27] The National Center for Education Statistics doesn't break these numbers down the way I'd like, but I can assure you that part-timers (sometimes called the burros of academia) primarily inhabit the public sector.[28]

Many teachers working on part-time contracts or as adjunct faculty without a long-term contract love their students and do a terrific job. But they are overworked and underpaid. They seldom have much institution-specific knowledge or much incentive to stick around after class to give students advice. Studies show that freshman students taking "gatekeeper classes" with adjuncts are less likely to return the following year.[29] At community colleges, the higher the percentage of adjuncts, the lower the graduation rates.[30]

Facilities and faculty tell only part of the story. The selective privates invest more heavily in student support and supervision than the publics do. I can't find numbers to document this claim, but I've talked with many parents and students who believe it to be true. It's also consistent with my personal experience. When I taught at Bowdoin College (whose tuition was $43,950 in 2008), I was required to send a pink slip to the dean of students if any student was failing, or even performing below my expectations, within the first six weeks.

Upon receiving that pink slip, the dean of students (a handsome, athletic, and enthusiastic young political scientist) would call the student to his office to ask what was going wrong. Talking things over, Allan would decide if the student needed a gentle nudge or a stern warning. He would also ask if he or she needed to see a tutor or a therapist. Those in serious trouble could be encouraged to drop out, take the semester off, and return when they were feeling better.

Not even the varsity athletes enjoy this level of solicitous attention at UMass Amherst. Although we try to reach out to our students, we don't have the resources to go beyond the basics. I once sat through an orientation session for potential students and their parents in which an assistant dean proudly declared that no one will ever get lost at UMass if they know which door to knock on. He never explained which door that was (certainly not his own). I entertained myself with an effort to calculate just how many doors there were on a campus used by over 25,000 students, imagining a new variation of the TV show *Survivors*.

We take pride in the ability of our graduates to cope with institutional dysfunction and navigate bureaucracy. Can't get the courses you need through the online registration system? Set your alarm for 2 A.M. and get online just as the adds and drops from the previous day are being cleared. Is the light turned off in the undergraduate advisor's office? That's just because she is trying to fend off interruptions while she does her paperwork. If you knock long enough and hard enough she will eventually let you in.

Our attrition rates are lower than average for public universities—about 67 percent of our entering class graduates within five years.[31] Still, I wish I knew more about that other 33 percent.

PRIVATE RIDES

Most selective private colleges and universities cost far more than public ones. Surprisingly, most are also a better deal for students in the sense that they provide a greater subsidy. The difference between what students and their families pay for and the amount spent per student is greatest at the selective privates. Some economists describe the financial aid offered to low-income students with terrific grades and high test scores as a kind of "wage" that is used to persuade them to attend: peers as well as teachers educate, and the promise of surrounding talent helps attract students whose families can actually pay the sticker price.[32]

On average, students at privates and publics get about the same amount of help from someone outside their family—calculated at about $8,200 in 1995.[33] This comes about for two reasons. First, many students at private schools have access to public financial aid. For another, they enjoy a subsidy from private school endowments: charitable gifts invested in stocks, bonds, commodities, real estate, and—increasingly—hedge funds yield income that these schools use to keep their tuition and fees well below the amount they actually spend per student.

Both subsidies come at considerable cost to taxpayers: when more financial aid goes to students at private schools, less is available for students at the publics. Also, all income from private-school endowments is exempt from taxation. The educational institutions that compete with public universities are private nonprofits that operate as charities even though they charge a hefty price. Contributions made to even the most expensive schools are tax deductible.

In general, the more expensive the school, the higher the subsidy to the students who attend. In 1995, students attending the wealthiest 10 percent of colleges got subsidies averaging $22,800 apiece, while those in the bottom 10 percent got a break of just $1,800. Williams College boasts a sticker price of about $40,000 per year, but spends about $80,000 per student per year.[34] At UMass Amherst, in-state students in 2007–2008 faced a sticker price of $17,399; expenditures per student came to about $19,262.[35]

Much of the aid at private schools comes from their endowments, which generate large amounts of tax-free income every year. But the schools also reap large amounts of public subsidy. More than half of Massachusetts state scholarship aid goes to students attending private colleges and universities. Between 2000 and 2007, the legislature beefed up financial aid for private schools even while reducing aid earmarked for needy students at UMass.[36]

Taxpayers further subsidize private schools by exempting their income and wealth from taxation. The estimated value of Harvard University's endowment in 2007 was $34.9 billion. In that year it enjoyed a 23 percent rate of return, or about $8 billion in tax-free income.[37] If the state had taxed that income at 16.3 percent, it could have covered the entire cost of public higher education in the state in the same year (about $1.3 billion).[38] And that's not even counting the value of the property tax exemption on the real estate that Harvard owns in Boston and elsewhere.

Like other private universities, Harvard took a big hit when the stock market declined in the summer and fall of 2008. Between July and August, its endowment lost 22 percent of its value—about that same amount that it had earned the year before.[39] This financial instability is scary, and is especially threatening to private schools with smaller endowments and more precarious revenues. But it doesn't alleviate my frustration with the low level of support for public higher education.

Most of the experienced advocates for UMass explain that private schools like Boston University and Boston College have consistently lobbied against higher funding for the state system, which competes with them for in-state students. Harvard and MIT obviously have far less to fear—they skim from the nation's crème de la crème. The less prestigious privates turn away plenty of students, but they are, after all, rated higher the more they turn away. Of course they want more state support for higher education. They just want it to come through them.

MUSICAL CHAIRS

Students who are pretty confident that they can get through college should definitely get onboard. Any financial planner could make the case for taking out whatever loans might be required to attend a public institution of higher education.[40] But if economic incentives were enough, high school and college graduation rates would have increased steadily over the last twenty-five years. They have not.[41] The number of students who aspire to college has gone up, but the percentage of individuals with college degrees is smaller among those aged 25–34 than in my generation of 45–54-year-olds.[42]

Conservative economists attribute this problem to "the breakdown of the American family."[43] But the families that have the hardest time getting together and staying together are precisely the ones who failed to graduate from college. As earnings stagnate for the bottom two-thirds of earners without college degrees and college costs continue to increase, the youth from these families obviously find it harder to pay for school.[44]

The weird pricing of higher education doesn't hurt everybody. The really rich (in money or influence) do just fine. So too do the really smart (or really talented in some other way), who essentially get paid through financial aid to share their intangible wealth with those less fortunately endowed. It's everybody else in the lower sectors of "quality space" that get run ragged: parents who feel like they can't afford what their children really need; young adults who fear they have already let themselves and their parents down. The financial aid system offers just enough to make many students feel that if they don't get what they need, the fault must be their own. And yet they try to be good sports, playing this knockabout game of musical chairs to the same old tune—a broken record—in the dark.

The Advisory Committee on Student Financial Assistance of the U.S. Department of Education calculates that financial barriers prevented between 1 million and 1.6 million college-qualified students from low- and moderate-income families from earning bachelor's degrees in the 1990s. Their prediction for the 2000–2010 decade: an additional 1.4 million to 2.4 million students.[45]

5

THE PIPELINES

Economies rely on circular flows, channeling inputs to produce outputs which in turn produce new inputs. Only part of this flow shows up in national income accounts because much of it involves the creation and nurturance of an input that is no longer bought and sold but only rented: human capital. Accounts of admissions at highly selective institutions often describe the flow of college students in bucolic terms as a mighty river.[1] In the public-sector institutions that educate 74 percent of college students, a more industrial metaphor is common: the pipeline. This image calls attention to human construction rather than force of nature: the hydraulic human capital system in which I serve a minor role as pump and filter as well as imaginary engineer.

The mostly below-ground plumbing, shaped by a hodge-podge of conflicting interests, is hard to figure out. Leakage is high even though a lot of liquid gets moved to a higher level. In parts of the system, the pressure seems too low, but in others it is way too high. Most academics seem fascinated by the distillation apparatus at the very top, designed to bottle the very best of what comes through. I don't like to crane my neck and would rather try to understand the system as a whole.

THE MILLION-DOLLAR PROMISE

The promise of a payoff provides a kind of suction that helps move students along. A college degree may not guarantee prosperity, but it will significantly reduce the probability of poverty or unemployment. Over the last twenty years, Americans without a college degree have found it harder and harder to find decent jobs. A report published by the National Center for Public Policy and Higher Education puts it this way: "Education and training beyond high school is no longer discretionary for those who aspire to full social and economic participation in American life."[2] Translation to less lofty language: If you don't get a college degree, you will get nickled and dimed. You will work long hours for crummy pay without any benefits. You will lose your job easily and often, and won't be able to help your own kids pay for college.

Strong evidence supports the "college or else . . ." argument. In 1980, the college premium for full-time year-round workers, both men and women, was about 50 percent. By 2000, that premium had doubled, meaning that over a lifetime a college graduate could earn about twice as much as a nongraduate—say an average of $60,000 instead of $30,000. Over a career of forty years, the difference adds up to more than a million dollars. College has become the new high school, the gateway to a more lucrative credential. The big bucks come from professional degrees, which offered about another doubling of lifetime income over that of a mere bachelor's.[3]

Much of this difference is driven by the decline in income of those who didn't complete college rather than an increase in the income of those who did. As Figure 2 shows, those who didn't attend at least four years of college (the bottom line trending down) had lower incomes in 1990 than their counterparts in 1963. Those with four or more years of college in 1990, on the other hand, were significantly better off than their counterparts in 1963 (the top two lines, trending up). In other words, they gained not only relative to others, but also in absolute terms. Measured in terms of real income, these workers were substantially better off in 1990 than their counterparts were in 1963.

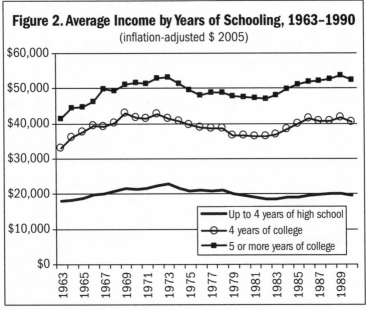

Figure 2. Average Income by Years of Schooling, 1963–1990 (inflation-adjusted $ 2005)

Legend:
- Up to 4 years of high school
- 4 years of college
- 5 or more years of college

Source: U.S. Census Bureau, "Years of Schooling Completed—People 25 Years Old and Over by Median Income and Sex, 1963–1990," available at http://www.census.gov/hhes/www/income/histinc/p17.html.

Why pause in 1990? Only because the Census Bureau improved the way it measured education in that year, shifting from years of education to completion of a degree. The trends in this measure, from 1991 to 2007, confirm the "you should stay in school or else" story (Figure 3). But this figure shows that the gains are relative rather than absolute. Sure, the differences remain, but none of the lines are heading up. Young people need to run faster and harder just to stay in place. A 2006 CNN poll made much of the fact that over 60 percent of American adults without a college education agreed that "it is impossible for most Americans to achieve the American Dream," while only 38 percent of college graduates agreed.[4] A lot depends, I guess, on how that dream is defined.

Sometimes advocates for higher education make it sound as if a degree itself will generate a higher salary. But the law of global supply and demand represents a higher power, and productivity often matters less than one's place in line. In the late twentieth century, many other factors increased the demand for educated workers more than the supply. Now, supply as well as demand is ramping up. Students everywhere, such as those at Keene State described in chapter 1 who observed "someone's got to work at Starbucks," can sense what's going on.

PRODUCTIVITY AND INEQUALITY

Still, there's a puzzle here. Our gross domestic product has been growing at a steady rate, and we know a lot more than our parents did. Most of us now own computers, cell phones, and DVD players and know how to Google an answer to almost any question. We live in the most affluent, technologically advanced economy in history and know how to troubleshoot and multitask and work long hours. You'd think that most of us with diplomas could also report a steady increase in our earnings compared to the previous generation. Yet the income of the average college graduate has failed to keep up with gains in overall productivity.[5] In 2004, the average man in his thirties earned less in 2004 than his father did in 1974, after inflation.[6] Without increases in women's hours of paid work, which generated more market income, their families would also have been worse off.

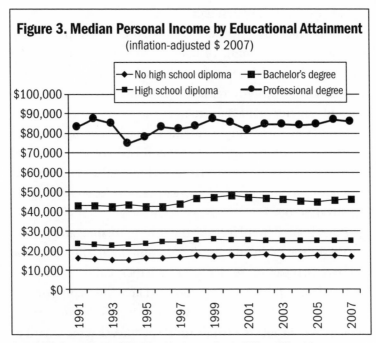

Figure 3. Median Personal Income by Educational Attainment
(inflation-adjusted $ 2007)

- No high school diploma
- High school diploma
- Bachelor's degree
- Professional degree

Source: U.S. Census Bureau, "Educational Attainment, People 25 Years Old and Over by Median Income and Sex, 1991–2007," available at http://www.census.gov/hhes/www/income/histinc/p16.html.

The pipes have both narrowed and lengthened. Income inequality has been increasing over time, channeling the benefits of productivity gains (as well as tax cuts) to the very top. Conservative economists argue that growing income inequality has an upside: it rewards those who try harder and entices more kids into college.[7] But increased income inequality in the United States has not been driven by the differences between those with college degrees and those without. The masters of the universe with incomes of more than a million a year, otherwise and approximately known as the top 1 percent, have enjoyed by far the greatest gains.[8]

I can't find any one study that reports where that group went to school (though, of course, some of them, like Bill Gates, are famous dropouts). Still, graduates of selective private schools are heavily represented in law, investment banking, and top-tier management.

Businesses increasingly recruit at these schools, and top students increasingly apply. As economists Robert Frank and Philip Cook put it, "The nation's elite educational institutions have become, in effect, the gatekeepers for society's most sought-after jobs."[9]

Talk about a circular flow: the shift of income and wealth toward the top of the income distribution in turn increased the ability of rich parents to richly educate their children, increasing the demand for elite education.[10] There are many parts of our economic plumbing that we don't yet fully understand and may not be able to change until we do. What's not hard to understand is how our system of financing higher education contributes to a cycle of increasing concentration of income, wealth, and influence.

THE HIGHER INEQUALITIES

Americans designed a variety of institutions to encourage upward mobility through higher education—public colleges and universities, the GI Bill, and financial aid. These institutions have had a positive impact but are no longer working the way they were intended. Most of the expansion of college enrollment has come from students in families that can afford to help them pay. Students from families in the top quartile are about three times more likely to graduate from college than those from the bottom quartile.[11]

In *The Shape of the River*, a now-classic book on admissions to selective universities, Bill Bowen and Derek Bok, past presidents of Princeton and Harvard respectively, called attention to low representation of students from low socioeconomic backgrounds. More recent research documents the extent of economic segregation. Within the top 146 colleges in the country, about three-quarters of students come from the top socioeconomic quartile, about one-tenth from the bottom half, and only about 3 percent from the bottom quartile.[12] Such differences in income and wealth have been intensifying over the past twenty years.[13]

Table 3. Median Parental Income for Dependent
Undergraduate Students by Institutional Sector, 2004

Private 4-year colleges and universities:	$67,534
Public 4-year colleges and universities:	$63,888
Public 2-year colleges:	$53,010
Private less than 4-year:	$47,279
Proprietary:	$36,469
All:	$59,505

Source: Calculated from the National Center for Education Statistics, 2004 National Post-secondary Student Aid Study by Tom Mortenson, "Class Segregation of Higher Education," postsecondaryopportunity.blogspot.com, May 24, 2006.

Inequalities are increasingly conspicuous within public higher education. Students from low-income families primarily attend two-year community colleges and proprietary schools, while flagship state universities (even those that barely rank within the top 100, like UMass Amherst) attract many from high-income families.[14] The median family income of students attending private colleges and universities in 2004 was not that much higher than the median for those attending publics: $67,534 compared to $63,888 (see Table 3). As middle-class students flee the higher costs of private schools, they apply to high-quality publics, crowding out low-income students.[15] In recent years, the public flagships have increased their aid for high-income students significantly more than for those with low-incomes. Even more startling is the fact that average institutional aid per high-income students is higher.[16]

Enrollment and graduation differentials based on class persist even when measures of talent and achievement are taken into account. The percentage of high-achieving students who do not enroll in college is five times higher among those who are poor than those who are rich.[17] One study of eighth graders sorted kids into groups according to their scores on a math exam. Those who ranked in the top fourth both on test scores and on family income had a high probability (74 percent) of finishing college. Their mirror-image group, with test scores and family income in the lowest fourth—had a very low probability (3 percent) of finishing college. The interesting results came in between: children who scored in the bottom quartile of test scores but the top quartile of family income were slightly more likely to finish college than their mirror image—at 30 percent compared to 29 percent for those in the top quartile of test scores but the bottom quartile of income.[18]

Note that the half-empty glass is also half full. Many kids from low-income families are smart enough to prevail, and many families with sufficient income can partially remedy the weaknesses of their children's eighth-grade math skills. So, it's not just the characteristics of the water—the individual units of human capital flowing through the system—that determine economic outcomes. The structure of the pipes obviously matters as well, which helps explain why educators spend so much time debating the kinds of filters they should use.

AFFIRMATIVE ACTIONS

The defining ideal of our educational system is meritocracy. Sure, we create an elite, but it is supposedly based on intelligence, talent, and hard work. The effort to demonstrate that merit is objectively and accurately awarded helps explain the rise of standardized tests, especially the SAT.[19] James Bryant

Conant, president of Harvard between 1933 and 1953, was the moving force behind development of the exam. He believed it would democratize education. As he put it, "Continuous perpetuation from generation to generation of even small differences soon produces class consciousness." [20] It wasn't entirely clear whose class consciousness he was talking about.

Increased reliance on SAT scores certainly allayed fears that elite schools were nothing more than agents of hereditary aristocracy. Ironically, however, the tests hardened the self-righteous self-confidence of those who relied on them as arbiters of merit. From the beginning, it was apparent that SAT scores reflected family background, race/ethnicity, gender, and class. Yet those who challenged the view that the scores represented some pristine, preexistent, and educationally consequential "intelligence" were treated as apostates. Efforts by the test's producer, the Educational Testing Service, to reduce background bias were quashed, as were more recent proposals to offer a kind of "discount" factor that would add additional merit to students from less advantaged backgrounds. [21]

The desire to believe that SAT scores provided an equitably tidy criterion for rationing access to top slots reached well beyond the circle of direct beneficiaries to become a defining principle of policies based on race rather than class. Anger that affirmative action for blacks and Hispanics resulted in acceptance of students with lower average SAT scores fueled the backlash against race-based affirmative action in the 1980s and 1990s. [22]

Most top private and public universities remained steadfast in their commitment to race-based affirmative action. They had never relied exclusively on standardized test scores or grades in choosing the country's potential leaders. Top athletes in team sports had long enjoyed a big boost. Still, admissions offices continued to emphasize the cold clear numbers as an antidote to concerns about political correctness. As competition for top slots heated up, well-heeled applicants began spending thousands of dollars on exam prep courses and coaches to help them present themselves in the best possible light. It was a regime, observed historian Jerome Karabel, "more successful in democratizing anxiety than opportunity."[23]

Ironically, SAT scores came around to bite top universities in the butt. The first hint of a reversal came when the federal Office of Civil Rights began investigating charges of discrimination against Asians at Harvard—a group of applicants with exceptionally high grades and test scores. In the process, they uncovered a different kind of affirmative action—preferences for children of alumni.[24] An enterprising *Wall Street Journal* reporter named Daniel Golden began following the trail. He won a 2004 Pulitzer Prize for a series of classic muckraking articles and followed up with a widely read and reviewed book, *The Price of Admission.*

Golden, the son of two UMass Amherst sociologists, himself a graduate of Harvard, combined quantitative analysis with anecdotal illustration. He found that at most Ivy League institutions, so-called "legacies" make up between 10 percent and 15 percent of every freshman class, a slice of the pie about equal to the 12 percent share of Black and Hispanic students. Explicit notes in admissions files often confirmed other evidence that preferences are especially generous for children of alumni who are celebrities or donors.[25] For instance, Republican senator Bill Frist sweetened the chances of his son's admission to Princeton with a $25 million contribution to his alma mater.

The response to Golden's revelations proves how precious that well-polished veneer of meritocracy had been. The *Harvard Crimson* denounced its university's policies, describing them as an "egregious vestige of aristocracy."[26] The conservative business magazine *The Economist* referred ominously to the "curse of nepotism."[27] Senator Edward Kennedy proposed legislation requiring universities to publish data on the racial and socioeconomic composition of its legacy admissions.[28]

The tone of educational policy debates began to shift toward more open advocacy of class-based affirmative action. Serious efforts to conceptualize such a major shift in admissions strategy had emerged as a response to the backlash against race-based affirmative action.[29] But if these proposals ever reached the table of the selective colleges and universities, they somehow got buried under the glossy alumni magazines. In *The Shape of the River*, Bowen and Bok had deplored the poor representation of students from low socioeconomic backgrounds in the highly selective colleges, but shrugged their shoulders when it came to remedies.[30]

Gradually, however, resolution to address the problem grew. In 2005 Bowen and two coauthors presented a detailed rationale for "a thumb on the scale" for students from low-income families.[31] They challenged the prevailing view that selective colleges were already doing as well as they could, comparing admissions rates among students with combined

SAT scores in the 1250–1299 range at nineteen selective institutions. Among those who were recruited athletes, 77 percent were admitted. Among blacks and Latinos, 66 percent were admitted. Among children of alumni and other legacies, 51 percent were admitted. Among those from nonminority low-income families, 37 percent were admitted—essentially the same rate as everybody else.

Meanwhile, Amherst College trustees welcomed a new president in 2003, Anthony Marx, who was passionately committed to recruiting more low-income students.[32] The college engaged its faculty and students, as well as its admissions office, in the process of rethinking its own priorities. In an effort to minimize the costs to members of its constituency—including athletes and alumni—the trustees laid out an ambitious fundraising plan to expand the size of the student body, resolving that bringing poor kids in would not shove rich kids out.

Pushed by Bowen and pulled by Marx, several of the most prestigious colleges and universities in the country improved their consciousness of class. Harvard University announced that it was suspending tuition and fees for students from families with an income of less than $40,000. Princeton promised to provide direct financial aid in lieu of student loans. So too did Yale, the University of Virginia, and the University of North Carolina at Chapel Hill.[33] Yet only the well-endowed institutions could afford this elegant gesture of noblesse oblige.

The symbolic change was certainly momentous. But down the road from Amherst College, where the UMass budget continued to take big hits, the lofty concepts were trumped by ugly numbers. About 430 students matriculate at Amherst

College every year, compared to about 4,500 at the University of Massachusetts. Overall, new policies at the selectives would do little to increase overall opportunities for low-income students to go to college. They would simply redistribute the brightest and the best, changing the composition of the elite stream. The pipes themselves would remain unchanged.

THE PLAYING FIELDS

Americans generally like the concept of equal opportunity but are not very good at explaining exactly what it means. Does it mean that everyone, no matter how humble his or her origins, has a chance to rise to the top? How big a chance does it have to be? One in ten? One in a hundred? One in a million? The "level playing field" is such a crazy metaphor. You're facing the New England Patriots on your own with a pigskin in your hand, but as long as they're not uphill, everything will be okay?

The more I worried about how to save UMass, the more the terms of the debate seemed out of date. Most people I talked to about it relied on a kind of litany of economic faith succinctly summarized by the current chair of the board of governors of the Federal Reserve Bank and professor of economics at Princeton University, Ben Bernanke:

Although we Americans strive to provide equality of economic opportunity, we do not guarantee equality of economic outcomes, nor should we. Indeed, without the possibility of unequal outcomes tied to differences in effort and skill, the economic incentive for productive behavior would be eliminated, and our market-based economy—which encourages productive activity primarily through the promise of financial reward—would function less effectively.[34]

Men in charge of really important things like the country's interest rates may not have time to update their political philosophy. But the comforting old distinction between equality of outcome and equality of opportunity has always left children (and college students) out of the picture. Sure, if you take adults as your starting point, you can distinguish between those two theoretical equalities. But outcomes for parents affect the opportunities available for their children.

Children don't choose the preferences or capabilities they develop. Their family background and early childhood experiences determine what they want as well as what they have. In recent years economists have grown more interested in the production of human capital, and a growing body of research reveals the impact of parental education and income on outcomes for children.[35] Nor are parents the only outside influence. Cultural norms, mass media, peers, and neighborhood characteristics channel them in ways over which they can't exercise much control.[36] Small initial differences in capabilities play back in ways that amplify preexisting inequalities based on race and ethnicity as well as class.[37] As conservative Nobel Prize–winning economist James Heckman puts it:

Never has the accident of birth mattered more. If I am born to educated, supportive parents my chances of

doing well are totally different than if I were born to
a single parent or abusive parents. I am a University of
Chicago libertarian, but this is a case of market failure: children don't get to "buy" their parents, and so
there has to be some kind of intervention to make up
for these environmental differences.[38]

Too bad children can't buy their own parents. Imagine
the glossy brochures, the application forms, the standardized
tests, the rankings of the country's best. If only time could run
backward, as in Philip Dick's *Counter-clock World*, where people grow young instead of old, and regurgitate food instead of
eating it. If you worked hard to earn a decent living, you could
look forward to a happy childhood. If you had your M.B.A. in
hand, you might look forward to ballet and horseback riding
at age ten.

Of course, most parents and children are genetically linked.
Maybe smart kids just get rich and then raise smart kids, who
in turn get rich. Some economists try to explain the rise of
Western civilization in these terms.[39] Others use this reason-
ing to argue that efforts to redistribute income to poor families
will have little effect, or that increased investment in higher
education won't pay off.[40] I think these arguments grossly
overstate the influence of genetic differences. But if they are
accurate, then young people's efforts are less important than
their endowments, and it seems especially cruel to justify extreme inequality as a spur to increased effort.

Bernanke asks us to choose between inequality and inef-
ficiency as though these are our only choices: capitalism ver-

sus communism, that old Cold War polarity. But we live in a world of mixed economies, and the question is not whether inequality in the abstract is acceptable but whether we can have too much of that presumably good thing. Many economists, including Robert Frank (a close friend of Bernanke's and coauthor of a textbook with him) argue that the winner-take-all dynamics of hypercompetition lead to wasteful arms-race dynamics.[41] They also tempt individuals into cheating and fraudulent behavior.

If the probability of success is too low, individuals may rationally opt for other strategies, such as slacking off.[42] My favorite illustration of this rather obvious point comes from an anecdote of game theory known as "pigs in a box." One pig in the box is big, strong, and fast. The other is small, weak, and slow. By pressing a lever on one side of the box, the pigs can cause food to be deposited on the other side. Every time the small pig depresses the lever, however, the big pig beats him to the food. The small pig soon learns to stand by the food chute, wait for the big pig to depress the lever, and grab a bite before the bigger pig arrives.[43] It joins the so-called underclass.

High levels of inequality undermine social solidarity, making it difficult to address problems that can't be solved by simply charging items to your credit card. They also breed a disabling cynicism that can be difficult to reverse. American optimism is not an inexhaustible resource. In March 2007, a Pew Research Center poll reported that 73 percent of respondents agreed with the statement "Today it's really true that the rich just get richer while the poor just get poorer."[44] I'd wager that their answers depend heavily on where they went to school.

HEREDITARY MERITOCRACY

Plenty of social science research tells us that economic plumbing matters, no matter what is flowing through the pipes. The strength of correlation between the educational achievement of parents and that of their children varies considerably across regions of the world: it is highest in Latin America and lowest in the Nordic countries, with the United States in between.[45] In the United States about half the advantages of having a high income are passed on to the next generation—significantly less mobility than Canada, Germany, or Denmark.[46]

A hereditary meritocracy is better than the plain old aristocracy that conservative William F. Buckley championed when he called for greater alumni preferences at Yale.[47] But it's not exactly the stuff of which new dreams can be made. An educational elite composed of varied backgrounds based on race and class (as well as many different talents) seems preferable to the plain old vanilla kind. But who determines the relative size and privilege of this elite? That job falls, at least in part, to the rest of us who choose to fund or not to fund our public schools.

6

THE BUSINESS MODEL

At a meeting with the faculty union Retrenchment Committee on June 11, 2003, the provost of UMass Amherst, Charlena Seymour, asked out loud, "Why can't we run the university like General Motors?" If you know something about the history of General Motors, or its growing problems over the past five years, you might find this question either sad or funny. Maybe the larger point was that we should try to be efficient. With that point, I agree. What I don't agree with is the presumption that we should maximize our profit.

Maybe the provost asked this question because she thought the faculty members had their heads in the clouds. I think what she meant was something like "Enough of this melodrama; let's get costs under control and report back to the shareholders." This view gained popularity in 2003, when Secretary of Education Rod Paige cited auto magnate Henry Ford to announce "Good schools operate like a business."[1] Yes, like a business—rather than, say, a hobby. Give me a choice between capitalism and feudalism, and I'll pick capitalism every time. But General Motors has gone bankrupt.

Protected for many years by its sheer size and political clout, the company made an amazing variety of mistakes. Its Corvair was so famously vulnerable in accidents that it prompted Ralph Nader to write *Unsafe at Any Speed*, the book that launched his career as a public-interest lawyer. In the 1980s the company's CEO, Roger Smith, refused an interview with a grungy journalist named Michael Moore and inspired the now-famous movie *Roger and Me*. General Motors' lack of interest in producing small, fuel-efficient, reliable, high-quality vehicles contributed to the global success of Honda and Toyota. A recent documentary, *Who Killed the Electric Car?* accuses it of prematurely discontinuing battery-driven transport, a technology that has recently been born again.

Businesses understand the concept of sticker shock, so the business model for higher education deserves serious consideration. The question is, which business model? In an industry like education, results are unpredictable and difficult to measure. As in no other industry, consumers are buying, in part, an evaluation of their own abilities that lacks credibility if all they pay for it is money. The consumers in this case are also producers; their intelligence and effort are among the most important inputs into the final product. Some parts of this process probably can be standardized enough to sell on a piece-rate basis, as the growth of online courses surely testifies. But running education like any other business creates temptations to engage in bad behavior—the kind of bad behavior that hurts a lot of people and ends up costing everyone a lot of money.

INCENTIVIZE, INCENTIVIZE

My colleagues in the English department wince at grammatical malpractice, but sometimes it's just a good idea to "incentivize." When my pet is good, I give him a treat; and if he's really bad, he gets a slap. Economics rightfully emphasizes the importance of motivation. But this emphasis is often interpreted in simplistic terms, as in "follow the money," "you get what you pay for," "just pay for performance." Hah. If it were easy to measure performance accurately and reward it fairly, there would be little need for managers or personnel departments, much less economists.

Sure, humans are motivated in part by money, and many of us like to goof off when we can. But if money was all we cared about, we would never raise kids in the first place—we'd stick all that money in our 401(k)s instead. Why would anyone primarily motivated by money go into teaching when they could earn at least five times more by going into investment banking, a job which is not demonstrably five times harder and, until recently, not terribly hard to get? Most people intrinsically care about what they do and how they do it, happily for the rest of us, who often find it hard to measure individual "value-added." Economic research—including results from carefully controlled laboratory experiments—shows that norms of reciprocity and fairness have a big impact on effort and efficiency in the workplace.[2]

Yet many people—and even some economists—seem to remain persuaded that the problem with public education is that it does not correctly "incentivize" teachers. This point of view comes through loud and clear in attacks on teachers' unions, often accused of selfish efforts to make life comfortable and easy for teachers. It also comes through in attacks on the public sector as a whole. Managers in the public sector are paid a salary whether or not their "firm" is losing money. So, the argument goes, they don't have an incentive to provide services in an efficient way. The *Boston Business Journal* once published an article by the chair of the economics department at Boston University entitled "No Reason for State Universities."[3] Let the state provide subsidies to students, he argued, and give them the freedom to shop around and take better advantage of institutions like his own (which, he seemed to imply, are run more like "businesses").

I don't see why private nonprofits should necessarily be better than public ones, or why either is necessarily any more bureaucratic than a large firm like General Motors. We should try to improve incentives wherever we can, but that doesn't lead to the conclusion that we should tie individual pay to individual performance. As a vast management literature shows, individualized incentives can undermine cooperation and teamwork. If I'm going to be judged on my performance in the classroom compared to yours, why should I help you learn to be a better teacher?

Some competition is good. Too much competition brings out the worst in people, tempting them to cheat or to abuse others or themselves. Routine use of steroids in competitive sports offers a poignant example of the temptation to mortgage one's future health in the hope of a big win. Of course, if everyone uses steroids, they don't even deliver a competitive edge; they just destroy every player's health. The business world offers plenty of examples of blowback from heated competition that stoked pursuit of individual self-interest. In 2001, managers at large accounting firms as well as at Enron were publicly exposed cooking their books to overstate their profits. In 2008, managers at major investment banks around the world were caught with their pants down, having exposed their investors to shocking levels of underreported default risk that created a global financial crisis.

THE BLUEBERRY PROBLEM

The risks of opportunism are particularly high in industries like education and health, where consumers, almost by definition, are unsure of what they most want and need. Even using the word "consumer" seems weird, since our society entitles all its citizens to at least some education and health provision. Are students the consumers, or are taxpayers, donors, and parents, who provide most of the financial support for education? Students are, in a sense, the "output" that we university professors are paid to produce. They are also the "input"—the raw material that we work with.[4]

Jamie Vollmer, a businessman turned education advocate, describes his efforts to persuade educators of the relevance of his experiences producing and marketing a very successful blueberry ice cream. His presentation was going well until a gray-haired woman at the back of the room raised her hand and asked him what he would do if he received an inferior shipment of blueberries. Anticipating her point, he still could not evade it. He conceded that he would send them back.

> "That's right!" she barked. "And we can never send back *our* blueberries. We take them big, small, rich, poor, gifted, exceptional, abused, frightened, confident, homeless, rude, and brilliant. We take them with

ADHD, junior rheumatoid arthritis, and English as their second language. We take them all! Every one! And that, Mr. Vollmer, is why it's not a business. It's school!"[5]

Apparently most people in the room, rallied by her comment, began shouting "Blueberries! Blueberries!"

This story stuck in my mind because I heard it just as I was struggling with a problem in the economics department at UMass. We had too many economics majors for the number of faculty available to staff the required courses. We had reason to believe this would be a long-term problem, and began to discuss raising requirements for entrance into the major. The management school sets a far higher bar for admission than we do. In fact, many of our students major in economics because their grade point average is not high enough to get into the management track. Why not ratchet our standards up?

One faculty member spoke out strongly against this option. He didn't directly invoke the blueberry problem, because, unlike public primary schools, we can turn students away. Instead, he pointed out what would happen if every department on campus responded to the shortage of resources by raising standards for admission to the major. A lot of students who had been admitted to the university would, in effect, be denied the opportunity to take advantage of it. We decided against this strategy, and later learned that the provost took steps to prevent other departments from implementing it as well. The management school, however, continues to enjoy the prerogative of selecting the highest grade of fruit.

A simplistic application of a business model implies that the outcome of the education process is . . . a standardized test score. Many teachers, however, cling to the romantic notion that the goal is to develop individual capabilities.[6] Teaching students a set of facts—or even analytical problem-solving methods—is far easier than teaching students to become self-motivated lifelong learners. Both are hard, so if you tell teachers all you care about is their students' performance on standardized exams, you will likely encourage them to devote more energy to the first task rather than the second. If test scores go up as a result, has the quality of the output increased? Sure, if you have defined output in these terms. It's kind of an accounting issue, isn't it—just like the one that Enron faced?

Teaching evaluations offer another example of measurement and accounting problems. They provide useful but limited information. The average scores that are typically reported often obscure qualitative differences. Sometimes a teacher who gets mediocre scores overall has a transformative impact on a small number of students. Evaluations of teaching in small classes, where there is opportunity for personal interaction, are typically higher than those for teachers in large classes, where it is easy to fall asleep. Teachers who grade in a generous and forgiving manner tend to get higher evaluations than those who set strict standards.[7] Physically attractive teachers get ranked more highly than the homely. Sex appeal plays a big role on rateyourprofessor.com, with hot-pepper icons awarded to those considered hotties.

In other words, it's hard to pick good teachers simply by the numbers. The same is true of corporate chief executive officers (CEOs). Every year, *BusinessWeek* publishes an analysis of the performance of most highly paid CEOs, examining the relationship between pay and quantitative measures of performance. The editors always remark on how weak the relationship turns out to be. Many unmeasured, unpredictable factors—like the sudden run-up in oil prices in 2008—affect economic outcomes.[8] The only workers in the United States who are literally "paid for their performance" are those who earn a piece-rate (like a dollar for picking a bushel of tomatoes) or a sales commission. Even in those instances, much depends on the characteristics of the field or store they work in.[9]

Still, the idea that teaching should be a popularity contest prevails. Recently, the Texas Agricultural and Mechanical College decided to award bonuses to instructors of up to $10,000 based on student evaluations—over the protests of many faculty who had already won teaching awards.[10]

MORAL HAZARDS

The term that economists use to describe economic incentives that tempt people into bad behavior seems apt enough: moral hazard. Rewarding teachers and students without evaluating their performance in any way at all probably invites shirking. But rewarding them for the wrong things—even if those things can easily be measured—can also create a moral hazard. Such policies encourage workers to shift their effort toward the measured outcomes, to "game" the assessment.[11] Too much accountability—if it is the wrong sort—can be just as bad as not enough.

My A-list of moral hazards in higher education was inspired by many accounts of what has been going on in primary and secondary education as a result of the federal No Child Left Behind Act, which puts tremendous pressure on schools to meet quantitative standards of performance.[12] Among the examples: the New York City school system has been accused of pushing struggling students out of the system so they won't be counted as "dropouts."[13] A detailed quantitative analysis of the Florida Comprehensive Assessment Test found that schools gamed the system by manipulating the test pool.[14]

The very problems of public higher education described here and in earlier chapters have expanded the market for for-profit universities. Long before it collapsed in the summer of 2008, the investment firm Lehmann Brothers published a report noting that the reduced purchasing power of financial aid was creating a fabulous new market for entrepreneurs willing to move into the higher education field.[15] A range of different business models emerged. Some of them were not so bad, but the worst ones provide a telling illustration of how bad behavior can be incentivized.

From the point of view of an individual seeking the increased employment opportunities that educational credentials can provide, the most cost-effective solution in the world is the simple purchase of a degree. Just Google the phrase "free college diploma" and you can shop until you drop. The *Chronicle of Higher Education* refers to online diploma mills as the University of Spam.[16] These diplomas are not quite free, but you can pay for them with your credit card or just hand over the financial aid that eager entrepreneurs will help you apply for.

Strict regulation—known in this industry as "accreditation"—means that such diplomas are worth nothing to fully informed consumers or employers. But not everyone is fully informed, especially those who lack a college degree themselves. Many diploma mills claim to be "fully accredited" by an association that they themselves invented.[17] Aggressive telemarketing by salesmen practiced at "selling the dream" targets low-income students, who (like their "teachers") seldom face any negative sanctions. Only a few states make it illegal to use such degrees to get jobs or promotions—the others leave it up to employers, whose only option is to fire the worker who wouldn't have gotten the job in the first place without the fake credential.

One layer up from the scum at the bottom of this barrel lie institutions that practice a more subtle scam. They provide some bona fide educational services but enroll students most eligible for federal financial aid and least likely to make any demands. Careful tutoring in how to apply for grants and loans generates money up front.[18] The analogies with our problematic health care system are striking: health-maintenance organizations (HMOs) have a financial incentive to enroll only healthy individuals, known as "cream-skimming," just as education management organizations (EMOs) have an incentive to enroll the students least likely to impose costs, as in generating homework or tests that must be graded. In street language, this leads to "bottom-feeding," as in fish like carp. A volunteer group that monitors for-profit educational institutions calls itself Carpmasters.

In some states such as New York, commercial colleges be-

came so successful at recruiting low-income students by promising financial aid that they absorbed a large share of all federal
and state tuition aid without generating the results necessary
for students to pay back their loans.[19] Recruiters were often
awarded bonuses based on how many suckers they could sign
up. That practice has now been outlawed, but several whistle-
blower lawsuits charging companies with breaking that law
have recently been filed.[20] The more students who drop out or
fail to complete the course, the lower the costs. When students
default on their loans, taxpayers foot the bill. Both dropout
rates and default rates are high.[21] State and federal regulators
try to police the industry, but they are often outgunned and
outlobbied. Schools that are shut down in one state often pop
up in another under a new name.[22] These business enterprises
(unlike public universities) are free to spend their money con-
tributing to the political campaigns of key members of Congress.[23] And spend it they do, as strategically as possible.

Not all for-profit educational institutions follow the
bottom-feeder model; some enforce higher standards to market a higher-quality product. But the financial temptations of
malfeasance are high. Many honest managers and investors
seem to have been seduced by their ideological commitment
to the matchless virtue of the market. Among them is the former governor of Massachusetts, William Weld, who took little
interest in public higher education in the state while in office
between 1991 and 1997. He soon grew bored with his entire
job and left early, hoping for an appointment as ambassador
to Mexico. In 1999, an investment group he helped manage
invested heavily in for-profit education, with Weld himself

proclaiming that "changes in education are coming as surely as the Berlin Wall went down."[24]

Two companies that his group invested in were shut down by allegations of fraud, effectively ending Weld's political career. The first company, Franklin Driving School, was closed by the state of Kansas after its own insurance company complained that its practice of hoodwinking vulnerable job seekers was leading to unacceptably high loan default rates.[25] Despite this experience, Weld agreed to serve as CEO of a second for-profit education company, Decker College, at an annual salary of $700,000 per year. Complaints about the quality of the program soon surfaced, publicized by a local reporter in the Louisville *Courier-Journal*. Both the U.S. Department of Education and the state of Kentucky took actions that effectively closed the school less than a month after Weld resigned as CEO.[26]

Since 2006, attention has shifted away from for-profit schools to for-profit student loans. Many financial institutions made contributions or other kinds of sweetheart deals with colleges and universities to channel student borrowers toward higher-cost lenders.[27] The secondary market for student loans operated much like the subprime mortgage market, where creation of extra debt combined with the off-loading of risks generated extraordinary profits. In this case, however, 90 percent of the loans made were guaranteed by taxpayers, yielding even greater windfalls. The government ran a direct loan program that provided the same lending services for about half the cost, but its scope was purposely limited to leave more room for the private sector.[28] There's a technical name for this: boondoggle.

INVISIBLE QUALITIES

Like many counterparts at other large public universities, administrators at UMass Amherst have embraced the logic and language of the business model. We are urged to cut costs and increase revenues. One way to accomplish this is to lower quality in ways that the "customers" won't notice. It's called adulteration. Millers figured out how to do it long ago by putting powdered clay in the flour; similarly, drug dealers sometimes add baby powder to their products. Quantity can be manipulated, too. When soda companies increase the price per ounce, they either keep the price the same and lower the quantity in the bottle or increase the price proportionately more than the size of the bottle, to make the price increase seem less salient.

Consumers are not dumb. They often notice and respond to changes in the things they buy on a regular basis. They exercise some sovereignty there. But higher education is often a one-time purchase, and assessment of its quality is an industry in itself. More credentials and high-status research doesn't necessarily contribute to better teaching. Some part-timers and adjuncts offer exceptional talents in the classroom, but it takes time and commitment to develop and improve the teaching of a department or school as a whole, along with incentives to contribute to the collective product.

Look at the private liberal arts colleges that represent the acme of high-quality higher education, and you will find that most faculty are in tenure-track or tenured positions. Very few are hired on a per-course or per-semester basis as so-called adjuncts. Private research universities such as Harvard, Princeton, and Yale rely heavily on graduate students, but they don't hire many adjuncts either. By contrast, at the largest for-profit university in the country, about 95 percent of instructors are part-time.[29]

Public universities are moving toward the for-profit model, with the proportion of courses taught by adjuncts rising steadily over time. Even some private universities (outside the top tier) are moving in this direction. As a result, the average for higher education as a whole is going up. Between 1976 and 2005, the number of full-time tenured or tenure-track faculty increased by 17 percent, while the percentage of full-time non-tenure-track faculty increased 223 percent, and the percentage of part-time faculty increased 214 percent.[30] A recent quantitative analysis suggests that such changes lower expected graduation rates, especially at public institutions.[31]

The "pseudo-market approach" is undermining tenure, professionalism, and the quality of education at public institutions.[32] At UMass Amherst, the number and the percentage of tenure-system faculty fell dramatically between 1986–1987 and 2004–2005, from 1,215 to 865. The size of the student body stayed about the same.[33] In public hearings—and on a DVD produced to help the faculty union lobby the state legislature—both faculty and students testified to the negative impact on their working conditions and educational experience. As activist efforts publicized this information, public opinion toward increased funding shifted in a more positive direction (see discussion in chapter 8).

But potential undergraduates can't easily see or assess these changes. For example, guides to colleges and universities typically report the ratio of students to faculty. The *U.S. News and World Report's Ultimate College Guide*, an impressive, four-inch-thick compendium, reports this ratio of students to instructors as 8 to 1 at Amherst College and 17 to 1 at UMass Amherst.[34] What they don't tell you is that virtually all courses at Amherst College are taught by tenure-system faculty, while less than 60 percent of students at UMass Amherst are taught by such faculty in a given semester. What can students see when they check out our campus? Some attractive new dormitories, a new recreation center going up, and many beautiful welcome banners saying "Students First!" So much for truth in advertising.

Several years ago, when I was serving as department chair, I did not have enough money in my budget to hire the part-time or adjunct faculty we would need to provide our basic course listing for the fall semester. I was told the money was simply not available. Then, a week before classes started, I was offered what was essentially an opportunity to engage in venture capitalism. I would post several new courses, and the department would be paid (by the university) for them on a per-student basis. If at least twenty students enrolled, despite the late notice, our costs would be covered. If fewer than twenty students enrolled, the department would lose money (it would be subtracted from our spring budget). If more than twenty students enrolled, the department would retain the "profits."

I guess the assistant provost thought that the department chairs needed to be incentivized. The drama was heightened by the fact that the entire university software management system, subcontracted out to a private firm called PeopleSoft, malfunctioned so extensively that students couldn't see new course listings, much less register for them, until two weeks into the semester. The shortage of courses was so pressing that the courses I risked departmental "venture capital" on became overenrolled, and I made the department a modest pile of money (enough to staff three extra courses in the spring). But I had to hire part-time instructors at the last minute, with little opportunity to choose among them. I think some of them were pretty good, but however talented they were, they only had a week to plan their courses.

This story helps explain why undergraduate economics majors at this university are a pretty unhappy bunch. Our Office of Institutional Research posts huge spreadsheets online that report the results of surveys of undergraduates from 2003–2005. Eight questions were asked, but the last one is the touchstone: On a scale of 1 to 4, "What was the quality of your overall experience?" Over those three years, we ranked dead last in the university as a whole. A closer look showed that the quality of our teaching was ranked quite high, but our students were disgruntled because of poor access to courses and inaccessibility of faculty. Those are factors over which we have little departmental control. The way to "incentivize" us would be to give our department the resources we need to do our job and then monitor and reward our success in improving undergraduate education. I've seen little evidence, in recent years, of any such priority.

Quality is difficult, but not impossible, to measure. One instrument, the National Survey of Student Engagement (NSSE), provides substantive feedback on the quality of students' actual learning experiences.[35] Unfortunately, the national survey results are not published in one place, and schools themselves seem reluctant to emphasize them. No one—except those who come out at the very top—has much incentive to advertise complexity.

SELLING THE PRODUCT

The business model now pervades higher education, and is manifest in the high salaries and the vocabulary of college presidents and in the behavior of large nonprofits such as the College Board and the Educational Testing Service, which hold a near monopoly over the college admissions process.[36] Marketing is now big business among public universities, with new attention to slogans, brands, and mascots.[37] The University of Maryland famously increased its applications with a clever—and costly—public relations campaign.[38] As a postdoctoral fellow at Yale University, I was struck by the school's august slogan, *Lux et Veritas*. At the time, I thought it meant Luxury and Truth. It turns out that *Lux* just means Light. I recently learned of an upscale salmon store in Manhattan called Lox et Veritas, a lovely variation.

Our motto at UMass Amherst is plain English: Dream, Build, Achieve. It sure beats the mundane reality, which doesn't fit so easily on a poster: Apply, Pay, Try to Get the Classes You Need to Graduate. I've tried to learn how much we paid for the official sequence of three verbs, but with no success (none of my business, apparently). I did agree to participate in a teleconferenced "focus group" with faculty conducted by marketing consultants. They asked us, "If UMass was a person, who would it be?" Someone wistfully mentioned Henry David Thoreau; my equally implausible favorite was Jon Stewart.

The American Council on Education recently polled the public on the "brand images" of the terms "colleges and universities" and "higher education in America." The good news is that they polled pretty well.[39] I wonder how long that will last. Our main job now is to sell the product, for two reasons. First, if we can attract more out-of-state students, we can not only charge them more but maintain control of the tuition. This will make us less vulnerable to the boom/bust cycle of state revenues. At some schools, such as the University of Colorado at Boulder, out-of-state students represent less than 30 percent of the student body but generate more than 70 percent of all revenue.[40] You could call this "cross-subsidization," but retail sales managers use a different term: "cash cows." Out-of-state students yield our milk.

A second reason we need to sell the product is that it makes us look better, which in turn increases our political clout. If we get more applicants, we can turn more down, which in turn increases our quality rankings in *U.S. News and World Report*, the most influential annual assessment. These rankings influence state legislators, especially those taken in by the business model. One statistical analysis suggests that simply being included in the *U.S. News and World Report* rankings has a positive effect on state appropriations per student.[41]

The annual rankings are supposed to help students and their parents make good choices, and maybe they do. But in addition to nudging institutions to solicit larger and larger numbers of applications, they create a variety of perverse incentives. The single biggest weighting factor is a subjective ranking by administrators and officials at top schools. Woe to those who challenge their authority! Also, since average scores on standardized tests are factored in, test scores play an ever-larger role in both acceptance and financial aid. For these and other reasons, a small but significant group of liberal arts colleges recently announced that they would no longer cooperate with the ranking effort.[42]

The more expanded *Ultimate College Guide* published by *U.S. News and World Report* includes important information on better measures of quality, such as the percentage of first-year students who return and the percentage of students who graduate within four or six years. This is a useful guide, not merely a marketing device. But its usefulness is limited. As the economists who studied the impact of rankings on state legislatures noted, if it's cheaper to improve "on-paper quality" (as defined by the ranking method used by the magazine) than true quality, the effect of efforts to improve "on-paper quality" could be negative.[43] Ah . . . and who defines "true quality?" There's the rub.

Money, unlike quality, is easy to measure, especially if you have mastered math. Department chairs and program directors at my university were recently instructed to propose new hiring priorities as follows: "Every proposal must very clearly articulate the opportunity or payback underlying the proposed investment's value. The more direct the relationship, the better."[44] The proposed investment, in this instance, is a faculty member. I'm left wondering what kind of payback is intended here—probably patents or grants, since it's hard to assign a dollar value to the public good.

Universities now urge their faculty members to seek corporate sponsorship and privatize the gains from their research. Following the money often means abandoning any pretense of objectivity. It deincentivizes the pursuit of risky, creative ideas that have little chance of gaining funding.[45] It can also lead to downright corruption. Many studies document the impact of financial incentives on the results of drug trials, the development of new genetic engineering methods (in which genes themselves can be patented), and even researcher participation in insider trading.[46] If only the economics department could hire someone poised to discover exactly what institutional arrangements bring out the best in people. Surely someone would pay for that . . . or would they?

ONLINE EDUCATION

Sadly, bad business models have shaped—and distorted—most efforts by universities to move their services online. Often the goal seems to be to increase revenue by setting up what is virtually a for-profit arm of a public university.[47] New information technologies have dramatically lowered costs in a number of industries. Consider the kiosks at airports where travelers can now check-in without talking to an agent. On average, the annual cost of such a kiosk is 25 percent of what it would cost to hire a human unit, and it replaces 2.5 employees.[48] Let's see . . . that makes it ten times more efficient. You can see why the idea of a teaching kiosk might appeal. You can also see why many faculty might fear that they will be replaced by streaming video.

Web-based instruction and online courses could significantly improve the quality and lower the cost of public higher education—but only if safeguards are put in place to avoid the kinds of perverse incentives that lead to lower quality, such as those described above. At many public universities, including my own, the prices of online courses are actually set higher than those of real-time classes, and financial aid is not available. The goal is not to promote quality or accessibility but to generate more revenue. As a result, many tenured faculty dig in their heels and refuse to collaborate with such efforts. At UMass Amherst, the administration offers financial incentives to individual faculty members to develop online courses (I know because I got some!), but departments as a whole are not offered sufficient resources to develop a consistent, high-quality online complement to their regular courses. Here again, the business model has gone awry.

FEUDALISM VS. CAPITALISM

At convocation and at graduation, faculty members look medieval in their black robes, velvet hoods, and silly hats. And like feudal lords, we often resist changes that might make us scramble to adapt. But most faculty enter academia out of a profound sense of commitment to valuable ideals, a factor that keeps the price of higher education low. In 2006–2007, the average full-time faculty member earned a little under $70,000 a year, considerably less than workers in private industry with the same degree.[49] Median pay for CEOs at the top 500 Standard and Poor-listed companies in the same year was $8.8 million.[50] This pay difference reflects differences in priorities as much as productive capabilities.

Universities can learn important lessons from successful businesses: short-run profits don't always lead to long-term success, different businesses require different models, and quality management requires teamwork and commitment. If education is a business, it's one whose product is enhanced human capabilities, not increased revenues. It's an enterprise that relies on the core values of honesty, curiosity, and commitment to the common good. If those core values are undermined, a lot of people will see the value of their personal investments decline. They will be left holding small pieces of paper decorated with portraits of ex-presidents who hoped for something more profound.

Dear Student,

Would you be interested in achieving an outstanding 4.00 GPA? Would you like to find out how to:

—concentrate when tired or bored;

—learn faster and reduce 3 times the time allocated for studying;

—prepare for lectures and learn at least three times more than the other students;

—get an "A" grade in every class;

—write effectively notes and optimize the time you spend taking notes;

—acquire Vital Techniques on combating test anxiety;

—increase your retention rate by as much as twenty times;

—prepare for a test and learn new test-taking techniques in order to ace it;

—never have problems with writing assignments;

—communicate effectively with your professors and peers;

—and much more.

If your answer to the above questions is yes then please respond to my e-mail. Have a very exciting and rewarding academic year!

Andy Hewitt, Ph.D.
Education Specialist

"The logic of managerial production renders irrelevant or unvalued the notion of higher education as a place for dissent and unpopular ideas, for creativity and the life of the mind, for caring and relationships, except as inefficiencies that will likely be deemed wasteful or unaffordable." —Patricia J. Gumport[51]

7

FISCAL HELL

"It's the budget, stupid." Yes, of course the state budget largely determines the resources available for public higher education. But what determines the budget? As I became more involved with the grassroots organizing effort known as the Public Higher Education Network of Massachusetts (PHENOM), I forced myself to look at the numbers and tried to distill them into a one-page handout. It was not a pretty sight. In 2006, the average Massachusetts taxpayer spent more on state police and "corrections" (i.e., prisons) than on public higher education in the state, and more than twice as much helping pay for the costs of the war in Iraq (see box on page 141). How could we change that?

Since the 1980s, the country has been in a state of permanent tax revolt. Any mention of increasing taxes on anyone, anywhere, at any time has been greeted by a dragon's breath of disapproval. State budgets are complicated, idiosyncratic, and difficult for those who don't work with them on a daily basis to understand. Poor reporting by local news media, many of whom have slashed their own reporting budgets, exacerbates the problem. In 2007, Governor Deval Patrick of Massachusetts, a likeable African American businessman widely considered advance guard for Barack Obama, proposed increasing tax receipts by promoting casino gambling in the state. When the legislature shot that down, he avoided making any strong commitments to alternative ways of raising revenue.

Facing a scary international financial crisis, the new president-elect promised to deliver considerable aid to the states, and everyone believed he wanted to help out public higher education with his fiscal stimulus. Nonetheless, projections of state revenues created an atmosphere of doom and gloom, not just in Boston but at many state capitals around the country. California—the epicenter of the tax revolt—proved particularly vulnerable. Unlike the federal government, states can't run a long-term budget deficit. When state tax revenues go down, state spending must go down, even as the needs of the unemployed, the poor, the sick, and the elderly go up. Public higher education, on the other hand, can theoretically go to hell and then come back again. Except that, this time around, it probably can't, which is why we need to address the fiscal crunch head-on.

THE TAX WE LOVE TO HATE

Ironically, most state tax revenue problems derive from revolt against a tax that states themselves don't even collect. Most homeowners pay real estate property taxes to the municipality in which they live to pay for services like police, fire, and schools. As the percentage of homeowners in the country has grown, so too has the percentage of individuals paying property taxes. The average tax paid is not terribly high, but it is a very visible tax, usually paid in a lump sum once a year.[1]

Why should "visibility" matter? If we all act according to

textbook economic models, it shouldn't, because we should all make efficient decisions based on perfect information. But in practice, visibility matters a lot. For instance, drivers using toll roads are far more sensitive to price increases if they have to fork over the cash than if they use an automated system like EZ Pass that bills them later.[2] People whose federal income tax is completely withheld from their paychecks notice those taxes far less than those who have to send the Internal Revenue Service a check before April 15.

The property tax is not merely noticeable; it's aggravating. Individuals don't have much control over it, because it's determined by the assessed value of their real estate, which often diverges wildly from the initial purchase price, especially in boom areas (like California or Massachusetts) in boom times (remember those?). For most of the twentieth century, most municipalities assessed property at a tiny fraction of its market value in an informal process over which local residents had some control. While this process provided a political buffer of sorts, it was also subject to influence-peddling and abuse.

In the 1970s many states implemented standardized rules that linked assessments to market value as measured by actual transactions. But while the tax became less arbitrary as a result, it also became less flexible. Taxpayers were left frighteningly vulnerable to the escalation of real estate prices in their communities.

The property tax came to represent the worst of both worlds: the authority of the government combined with the vagaries of the market. Ordinary people didn't view their homes merely as investments, and they were not planning on "flipping" them as prices went up. Later, financial markets would make it easier—perhaps too easy—for individuals to capitalize on increases in market value by taking out home equity loans. But in the 1970s, most people who bought homes hoped to live in them for a good long time, and high property taxes made it harder for them to pay their other bills. Elderly households on fixed incomes were particularly hard hit.

The changing geography of family life weakened incentives to invest in one's own community. Once upon a time, elderly people paying taxes on their property could anticipate that their own grandchildren might benefit. But increased geographic mobility and the advent of a national job market— especially for the well-educated—increased the likelihood that the younger generation would move away. An influx of both legal immigrants and undocumented workers amplified the differences between taxpayers and school users in many communities.

Compared to the population as a whole, our older and more affluent citizens are disproportionately white while are our younger and less affluent citizens are disproportionately black and Latino.[3] Racial/ethnic diversity in a community tends to reduce its willingness to invest in public goods.[4] Events in California, a state with a large and growing Hispanic population, foreshadowed national trends. When a state supreme court ruling dictated that tax revenues should be redistributed from rich districts to poor ones in 1971, political support for public elementary and secondary schools began to decline.

Yet the emerging tax revolt featured activists from both sides of the political spectrum. Some critics from both the left and the right advocated elimination or strict limitation of the property tax.[5] Left-wing critics were more likely to propose ways of reducing the regressive impact of the tax, which bit big into the living standards of those living on a low or fixed income, especially the elderly. They favored policies such as homestead exemptions (which would reduce tax liabilities for those living in their own homes), "circuit-breakers" (which would limit the liabilities of low-income families), and classification schemes which shifted the burden of the tax toward businesses.

Right-wing critics were more likely to emphasize that taxes in general were wasteful, inefficient, and unfair. Few articulated this vision more eloquently than Howard Jarvis, famous architect of legislation that capped California's property tax at 1 percent of assessed value and stipulated that assessed values could not increase more than 2 percent per year unless the property underwent a change of ownership. Proposition 13, passed with strong public support in a 1978 referendum, also made it difficult for the state legislature to increase any taxes in the future, requiring a two-thirds legislative majority in both houses. Average property taxes in California fell by more than 50 percent.

Proposition 13 became a model for similar efforts in other states. Almost two-thirds of the states (including Massachusetts) had adopted restrictions on spending or revenue generation by the end of 1982.[6] Copycats moved quickly, especially where they could take advantage of ballot initiatives. They were particularly successful in states where other measures to limit the impact of property taxes (such as exemptions and

"circuit-breakers") were negligible.[7] The burgeoning tax revolt definitely slowed the growth of local spending, particularly
on primary and secondary schools. The consequences for California were dramatic: its schools, once ranked among the best
in the country, soon ranked among the worst.[8]

But the tax revolt did not halt increases in local spending because most local communities have needs that their
residents want met—not just for schools but also for essential
services like fire and police and snowplowing—that cannot
be efficiently provided by the private sector. As a result, many
states stepped into the breach, increasing the percentage of
their own revenues devoted to local spending. This, in turn,
increased the fiscal pressure on states to come up with new
ways of raising taxes and cutting spending by, among other
things, defunding state universities.

The revolt against the tax we love to hate morphed into
a hate campaign against all taxes. The success of Proposition
13 inspired Ronald Reagan to lead the Republican Party in a
new, more assertively antitax direction. His success, in turn,
contributed to giddy confidence in a simple formula that began
to define the conservative identity. Even prominent business
leaders who worried about the resulting pressure on state spending
were warned off. When Arnold Schwarzenegger campaigned
for Reagan's mantle as governor of California, one of his advisors, billionaire investor Warren Buffett, advised him publicly
to repeal or at least revise Proposition 13. Laughing out loud,
Schwarzenegger announced, "I told Warren that if he men-
tions Proposition 13 again he has to do 500 sit-ups."[9]

SQUEEZING THE STATES

A similar story unfolded on the other side of the country in my adopted home state of Massachusetts. A California-inspired referendum—Proposition 2½—put new rules into place in 1980 setting a ceiling of 2.5 percent on the tax rate and limiting the rate of increase in total revenues to no more than 2.5 percent a year. Since estimated market values were going up, some towns had to lower their tax rates in order to comply with the second restriction. Between 1980 and 2008, the annual increase in inflation was lower than 2.5 percent in only seven years. Towns that had reached the 2.5 percent ceiling could increase revenues sufficiently to keep pace with inflation over the period only if they enjoyed new construction.

In small New England towns like the one I live in, budget decisions are made by local selectmen—essentially elected volunteers—who take on the contentious task of reconciling growing costs with revenues that cannot keep pace. Most debate at town meetings focuses on discipline and thrift versus responsibility to meet the needs of residents, especially children. But parents of young children are often underrepresented—the difficulties of balancing paid and family work leave them little time to participate. Local schools are left vulnerable.

The initial pain of Proposition 2½ was dulled in communities like mine by increases in state aid, raised in part by an income tax. This redistribution worked well in boom times, but income-tax revenues wax and wane over the business cycle. The slow growth of the late 1980s and early 1990s forced cutbacks in state aid. Some communities began the difficult process of challenging the restrictions with ballot overrides; small wealthy communities generally enjoyed more success than large poor ones.[10] Meanwhile, Massachusetts, like many other states, followed California's lead in moving toward more equitable funding of public schools with the passage of an education reform act in 1993. The state increased transfers to low-income districts, further buffering the negative effects of Proposition 2½. Local efforts to override the limits peaked in 1991, then subsided during the late 1990s (to blossom again during the 2001 recession, and most likely, in coming years).

But wherever the taxes moved, the tax revolters followed. Republican governor William Weld, elected in 1991, took advantage of a prosperous economy to promote nineteen tax cuts and—most important—to create momentum for a cut in the state income tax rate in 2000 after he left office. On the national level, politicians who raised taxes were swiftly punished. It is widely believed that the first President Bush failed in his reelection attempt because he raised the marginal federal income tax rate from 28 percent to 31 percent, even though this small change left Reagan's sweeping reductions largely in place (before Reagan came to office, the top marginal tax rate was 70 percent). President Clinton took even more flak when, in 1993, he raised the top rate to 39.6 percent. Less than 5 percent of taxpayers were affected by this change, but tax aversion proved contagious: close to 50 percent of voters polled believed their taxes had been raised.[11] The second President Bush pushed them back down again.

Efforts to squeeze government spending were not restricted to tax cuts. Congress began to devise new ways to off-load expensive programs on the states with so-called un-funded mandates. States were required to assume more finan-cial responsibility for the education of students with disabilities (Individuals with Disabilities Education Act); to perform extensive testing of students and monitoring of schools (No Child Left Behind Act); to improve accuracy, availability, and monitoring of voting machines (Help America Vote Act); and to improve homeland security—without any federal support. A large share of the cost of escalating Medicaid expenditures (the cost of providing health care to low-income families and long-term care to the elderly) has been borne by the states. The National Conference of State Legislatures estimates that the federal government shifted about $100 billion in costs to the states between 2003 and 2007.[12]

Federalism is supposed to increase flexibility, but perversi-ties abound. If a state reduces spending on Medicaid, it loses federal funds. By contrast, if it reduces spending on public universities, its residents gain eligibility for subsidized federal student loans and tax credits.[13] States spend more on prisons now not because of increased crime rates but because of lon-ger sentences and more restrictive parole policies for drug-related crimes. The now largely privatized prison system has no incentive to rehabilitate prisoners and get them out of jail because the industry reaps a large profit on them exactly where they are.

INSTANT MEGABUCKS

Largely blocked from tax increases, states began selling lottery tickets, a practice they embraced as a comfortable alternative to taxes. People gamble of their own free will, and perhaps the thrill of possibility itself makes their expenditure worthwhile. But lottery tickets are a stupid way to gamble because the expected benefits are so much lower than the costs—otherwise, the state would not make much money on them. Not surprisingly, college students spend a quarter as much money on lottery tickets as high school dropouts, and whites spend far less than African Americans and Hispanics.[14] Even in states like Massachusetts, where some lottery earnings are redistributed to low-income communities, the overall effect is regressive.[15]

Tax Ignorance to Support Education—not a bad slogan. Many states, such as Florida, Georgia, and Kentucky, developed dedicated lottery programs to support early childhood education and to help finance college financial aid. Similarly, many states devote cigarette tax revenues (as well as payoffs from tobacco firms delivered as part of a legal settlement against them) to good causes. But at least the tax on cigarettes discourages cigarette consumption. By contrast, most states, exempt from regulation under "truth-in-advertising" laws, actively promote lottery sales. Embarrassed by revelations of deceptive advertising by the state lottery commission, Massachusetts legislators tried to ban it from targeting poor communities through direct mail ads and to require it to communicate accurate odds of winning. Governor Weld vetoed their bill.[16]

Most economists agree that state lotteries represent a hidden sales tax.[17] No one makes you buy taxable items at the store, but when you choose to do so you are typically charged a sales tax calculated as a fixed percentage of the total. Likewise, when you buy a lottery ticket, a percentage of the price you pay—typically more than 30 percent—goes into government coffers. It just so happens that you are not told, up front, what percentage that is. Unfortunately, you probably need a college education to figure that out. And if you don't have one, you're not terribly likely to be informed on this issue or to vote on it, much less contribute money to a political campaign.

At least initially, lotteries helped states fund their schools. The trickling revenue gradually became a river. By 2006, ticket sales yielded a net income of more than $17 billion—enough, in principle, to finance public higher education in seventeen states, including Massachusetts.[18] Unfortunately, a significant proportion of lottery money earmarked for education is not actually spent for that purpose. Further, the lottery revenues make it easier for states to reduce other expenditures, neutralizing their net effect.[19] Today, state lotteries face increasing competition, not only from one another, but from other forms of legalized gambling like casinos.

These long-run changes, combined with the effects of recession, are further reducing funds available for higher education. My husband suggests that we devote the UMass sports arena to extreme gladiatorial sports and charge high admission to those who want to watch the administration and the faculty fight one another with wooden swords and catapults. As far as I know, this is still against the law. The new bucks will have to come from somewhere else.

A RECKLESS IDEA

Oh, wait, I forgot. Maybe we don't need new bucks. Maybe we can just keep on cutting taxes and force spending down to the levels a lottery can support. Support for Proposition 2½ has remained fierce even in this supposedly liberal bastion of a state. A referendum to eliminate the state income tax first went before Massachusetts voters in 2002. Advocates for its elimination refused to say what, exactly, should be cut other than that convenient abstraction known as waste. The income tax provides approximately 40 percent of all state revenues—a percentage that has increased steadily over the years as a result of property tax restrictions. Many voters who may have disagreed with its actual intent seized the opportunity to signal their dislike of taxes. As a result, the referendum almost gained majority approval, winning 45 percent of the vote.

In 2008, it was born again, with the high-priority-sounding name of Proposition 1. The cheerleaders estimated the average benefit to Massachusetts taxpayers—taxes averted—at $3,600. What they didn't say was that tax filers with incomes of less than $20,000 would enjoy a mere $240 savings, while those with incomes of more than $100,000 would enjoy between $15,000 and $16,000.[20] Most educators in the state—relatively well-paid earners who probably would benefit substantially from a tax cut—feared that it would cut our schools, from pre-K to UMass, off at the knees.

A newly formed Coalition to Save Our Communities mobilized activists (mostly teachers) to speak out, and I drove to Framingham with a colleague for a training session. The trainers discouraged too much discussion of who would benefit the most from the tax cuts, fearing that would prove divisive. They warned that the *Boston Globe* had published photographs of a fireman who was receiving disability lifting weights at a local health club. "Sure, there's some waste," we practiced say-ing, "but not that much." Our official slogan emphasized the need for caution: *Proposition 1: A Reckless Idea*. I didn't like the wording, because it made tax cuts sound like motorcycles or a one-night stand. But with the stakes so high, I wasn't about to defy the focus-group research.

This time around, in November 2008, the repeal effort won less than 30 percent of the vote. The financial meltdowns that dominated the news that fall discouraged the tax-cut ad-vocates. The claim that teachers, police, and fire protection workers were wasting money lost credibility with revelations of just how much of our taxpayer money bankers would need to bail out their sinking boats. Still, the results felt less like true victory than averted loss. The tax revolters had kept advocates for the public sector playing defense and blocked any discus-sion of how taxes might be raised.

TAX PAYBACK YEAR

What we needed were some new ideas for explaining why taxes aren't so bad—considering what they pay for. Conserva-tives celebrate something called Tax Freedom Day, a copy-righted concept based on the following hypothetical situation: if, starting January 1, you devoted your entire paycheck to up-front payment of your annual taxes, on what day would you finally be free of what you owe the government?[21] In 2008 that fateful day fell on April 23. Yes, taxes take a big chunk out of everyone's paycheck, more indeed than basic necessities like food, clothing, and housing. But conservatives make it sound as if the money goes into some secret vault where career bureaucrats gloat happily over the wasted spoils. They never mention what your taxes actually buy.

I decided to ask a hypothetical question of my own. What if Massachusetts residents who were twenty-two years of age and entering the labor market with a degree fresh in hand from our flagship university were asked to pay the state back for all the state and local expenditures on their education? How many years would it take the typical college graduate, earning a median income and paying the average combined state and local tax rate of 9.5 percent, to repay the Commonwealth, at a reasonable rate of interest? In other words, when would their Tax Payback Year roll around?

This hypothetical scenario is more complicated than Tax Freedom Day because it involves debt that is accumulated and paid back over time. But it is possible to estimate annual payments the same way that a bank charges for a mortgage, taking into account the amount and term of the implicit loan. From an accounting perspective, this approach assigns the benefits of average spending on education to the individual who directly benefits from it (rather than, say, to the parents of that child). This makes sense because not all taxpayers raise children, and those that do raise varying numbers of them. In this scenario, the state invests in children and expects repayment in order to finance ongoing investments in future generations.

By my calculations, the average twenty-two-year-old graduate of UMass Amherst would owe about $200,000 at graduation (the sum of average expenditures per pupil from the first grade on). Few individuals could fork this over right away because they are just entering the labor market. So, treat this sum like a mortgage that could be amortized over the next forty-two years (assuming an average life expectancy of seventy-five) at a 5 percent rate of interest. I used a Web-based home-mortgage calculator, www.mortgage-calc.com, to make this calculation, ignoring the cheerful advertisements promising me (in the midst of a global financial crisis) that I could get up to four loan offers within mere minutes. The monthly payments would amount to about $950 per month or $11,400 per year.

How many years would it take the average college graduate to pay that loan back, assuming that he or she paid 9.5 percent of his income in state and local taxes, entered the labor market in 2007 earning $30,000 per year (the median starting salary for college graduates), and enjoyed an increase in earnings of 5 percent every year (at this point in time, a rather optimistic assumption)? Almost thirty years. That is, at age fifty-one (about twenty-nine Tax Freedom Days later), this hypothetical college graduate will have reached Education Payback Year (not exactly Tax Payback Year, since other taxes and benefits belong in that equation). At that advanced age, individual taxes can start going toward paying back—and paying forward—the other public services people will take advantage of.

Ick! If you're the average reader, you didn't enjoy plowing through those tedious calculations. My point exactly! Benefits are harder to see, to measure, and to tally up than the taxes that we pay. Some people will obviously pay more taxes than others compared to the benefits they receive. Private insurance works the same way. People who get really sick enjoy a much better deal than healthy ones—measured in terms of dollars paid in to dollars paid out. The healthy are not oppressed by their good fortune, and, in my view, neither are the rich, though they pay more in taxes than the rest of us.

Most people have no idea what their taxes actually pay for, or what percentage actually lands back in their own pockets. Tell them about social policies in France or Sweden and they will proudly say, "Yes, but those poor European serfs pay higher taxes than we ever do." Yes, they do, but they also get more: reliable, efficient health care as well as access to virtually free public higher education.

Why can't most Americans accurately compare their real standard of living with that of people in other affluent countries? Economists don't make it easy for them, continuing to rely on measures of market income like GDP per capita that are terribly misleading, or tax rates that don't take the value of government benefits into account. The powers that be—including conservative media and think tanks—invest huge resources in public relations campaigns denouncing both public programs and progressive taxes. To better see through these complexities, people need—you guessed it—a darn good college education. Even more urgently, they need a clear and convincing explanation of how they can benefit from higher taxes to provide better health and education services.

SAY THOSE WORDS OUT LOUD

Yes, read my lips: higher taxes. During his campaign for president, Barack Obama proposed tax increases on families who make more than $250,000 per year. He also promised that no one would pay higher taxes than they did in the 1990s—returning to a top marginal tax rate of 39.6 percent.[22] Vice presidential candidate Joe Biden briefly got off the defensive, suggesting that higher taxes paid by the rich would be "patriotic." Republican vice presidential candidate Sarah Palin responded perfectly on script: "Raising taxes is about killing jobs and hurting small businesses and making things worse."[23]

Even as the financial infrastructure of deregulated capitalism crumbled, the tax revolt seemed like a train rolling down the mountain with a righteous faith in its own trajectory. That's because it always was based on something more profound than mere stinginess. It offered a larger cosmology of good and evil—an almost religious vision of how to keep bad things from getting worse. The basic principle of faith was Tax Cuts Good, Government Spending Bad. But the underlying theology was even more abstract: Private Sector Good, Public Sector Bad; Businessmen Good, Bureaucrats Bad.

Researchers have puzzled endlessly over why so many Americans have voted for tax cuts and other economic policies that offered them no obvious benefits and helped augment the wealth and income concentrated at the top of our economy. Maybe members of the white working class were so distracted by issues of race, gender, and gay rights that they forgot to pay attention to their pocketbooks.[24] Maybe they were both misinformed and disempowered by a political system that responds to financial contributions more than individual opinions.[25] Maybe the college-educated middle class was at fault, choosing to ally themselves with those above rather than those below them in the income distribution.[26]

The fog of public finance is even more difficult to see through than the fog of war. Perhaps many Americans have supported tax cuts for the rich not because they are indifferent to economic inequality, but because they largely fail to connect inequality and public policy. While politicians in the Democratic Party tend to favor public spending more than Republicans, they fear being accused of "class warfare." Yet awareness of class differences pays off: in states where legislators took action to protect low-income homeowners from skyrocketing taxes linked to increases in the value of their homes, efforts to impose limits on property taxes were often unsuccessful.[27]

Ironically, in the United States the tax revolt was actually reined in by its dependence on local ballot initiatives. In the United Kingdom, conservative prime minister Margaret Thatcher went too far too fast, abolishing the property tax altogether and replacing it with a poll tax so unpopular that it probably caused her downfall.[28] What might have happened in the United States if progressive advocates had developed and publicized a simple, consistent plan for a simpler, more equitable, and efficient system of taxation on the federal, state, and local level?

We will probably never know the answer to this question. But we will, over the next few years, be able to test another hypothesis: that economic inequality fed upon itself. The economic success of the very rich—their burgeoning incomes and lavish lifestyles—seemed to testify to their competence and expertise. When they promised that tax cuts would deliver prosperity to all, they told us something that we wanted to believe. After all, it had worked for them. Advocates for the public sector were easily labeled losers: Businessmen Smart! Bureaucrats Dumb! This ideological bubble stretched even further than the real estate bubble. Then, suddenly, both bubbles popped. It became apparent that we were all in one big bathtub, about to be sucked down the drain.

Spending Priorities in Massachusetts[29]

$918 Million:
What the Commonwealth of Massachusetts spent on public higher education in 2006.

$1.1 Billion:
What the Commonwealth of Massachusetts spent on police and corrections (the prison system) in 2006.

$2.6 Billion:
Average annual taxes paid by residents of the Commonwealth of Massachusetts to finance the Iraq war.

8

SAVING OURSELVES

It will be the goal of this administration to ensure that every child has access to a complete and competitive education from the day they are born to the day they begin a career. That is a promise we have to make to the children of America.[1]

—President Barack Obama, February 24, 2009

The Great Recession that brought the U.S. economy to its knees in 2008–2009 crippled both private and public university budgets. The value of endowments nosedived, forcing cutbacks even at the richest institutions.[2] The tremendous loss of both jobs and wealth made it difficult for parents and students to pay tuition bills. More students turned to affordable community colleges and state universities even as cutbacks in public support led to layoffs, program closures, and increases in tuition and fees.[3] While the Economic Recovery and Reinvestment Act funneled money to the states to buffer higher education against budget cuts, these funds were temporary and insufficient to compensate for the combination of long-run fiscal imbalance and crushing revenue shortfalls.[4]

Financial support for public higher education in the United States has declined largely as a result of distributional conflicts described in preceding chapters—the rich investing in political initiatives to reduce their federal income tax rates, employers successfully evading corporate income taxes, and many homeowners resisting property tax increases. A better understanding of this contentious process of modifying our social contract should enable us to bargain harder and smarter for a better one. We need to show Americans how increased public support for higher education can help us realize our best ideals and address some of the most pressing problems facing the global economy.

The Obama administration has made important headway on improvements in public higher education, and many states have implemented exemplary reforms. Still, these efforts remain fragmented and inadequate. I believe that advocates for public higher education should develop a plan to finance free public higher education for all who can prove that they will take good advantage of it. We need not just to save but to expand and improve our public education system.

FIRST STEPS

The Obama administration has provided families with more support to pay for college in the form of both financial aid and loans. The 2009 American Recovery and Reinvestment Act increased funding for the Pell Grant program—the primary source of need-based federal financial aid. Over the next two years, maximum Pell Grant benefits will increase 17 percent— the biggest boost in the program's history. The maximum grant of $5,500 in 2010–2011 should cover about one-third of the total annual cost of attending an average public university.[5] Increased eligibility means that families with incomes of up to about $50,000—about the median for U.S. households—may garner assistance.

The bill also boosts and improves income tax credits for expenditures on higher education. The new American Opportunity Tax Credit (similar in basic structure to the earlier Hope Credit) offers 100 percent reimbursement for the first $2,000 spent on higher education and 25 percent of the next $2,000 spent on qualified educational expenses. Most important, families that don't earn enough to pay income taxes—and that were therefore previously ineligible for an education tax credit—can earn a refund of $1,000, the equivalent of a straight subsidy. The credits can be claimed for a total of four years (they were previously restricted to two).

The stimulus bill also initiated major changes in student lending programs. The Federal Family Education Loan program, which offered private lenders subsidies to make guaranteed student loans, lost credibility in the face of major bank failures and bailouts. A spate of earlier scandals focused on improper gifts and incentives to university financial offices to give priority to some lenders over others.[6] Although a fight is shaping up in Congress at the time of this writing, most federally guaranteed student loans will probably be made directly by the federal government—with considerable cost savings to taxpayers.[7]

A new federal policy announced in June 2009 will dramatically reduce the burden of student loans. It allows anyone with a federal student loan to cap their loan payments at 15 percent of disposable income and pay nothing if their income is below 150 percent of the poverty line. It also forgives remaining balances after twenty-five years or, for those who choose to work in the public sector, after ten years.[8] This plan is modeled on policies developed in both the United Kingdom and Australia that have made loan payback contingent on future income.[9] Such policies have proved relatively popular and successful.

Changes in student loan administration will likely prove permanent. However, many of the other gains described here will either decline or lapse along with other fiscal-stimulus programs after two years. And many problems remain. The financial aid/tax credit approach to funding higher education is complex, confusing, and often poorly utilized. While steps recently taken to simplify the Free Application for Student Aid (FAFSA) form certainly move in the right direction, the overall hassle factor in paying for college remains high and probably discourages students from less-educated, low-income households.[10]

Budget shortfalls are forcing both public and private institutions to raise tuition and fees. While increased financial aid softens the blow, it also reduces political pressure to fight such increases. The differences between "sticker prices" and prices paid by those who garner aid will rise further. Families just over the Pell Grant eligibility line—in this case, about half of all U.S. households—may actually pay higher prices. Further, families that have saved for college and report "too many" assets on their financial aid forms will be penalized. This is hardly a recipe for mobilizing broad-based support for public higher education. A recent article in *BusinessWeek* noted that the increase in student aid will funnel large amounts of money to for-profit educational institutions designed to harvest it.[11]

STATE-LEVEL REFORMS

Many states have taken small steps in the direction of college as entitlement. The state of Georgia, hoping to promote economic development as well as expand opportunity, developed the Help Outstanding Pupils Educationally (HOPE) scholarship program, first established in 1993. This program uses dedicated lottery revenues to cover the costs of public higher education for all Georgia high school students who graduate with a B average, as long as they are able to maintain that average in their college work.

The program's simplicity and universality are appealing. It rewards students for working hard but doesn't set too high a threshold (about 40 percent of all high school students graduate with a B average or above). Students who elect to attend private schools can earn a subsidy toward their tuition and fees at those institutions of $3,000 per year. The program started out targeting low-income families but proved so popular that all income restrictions were soon dropped. Others states seem to like the idea—about thirteen have put similar, although typically more limited, programs into place.[12]

Critics point to some unpleasant unintended consequences of merit-based aid.[13] Students try to game the system by opting for easier classes, summer courses, or reduced course loads. Why should we care as long as they also study harder? Average high school grades increased faster and higher than standardized test scores, suggesting that secondary teachers felt some pressure to help kids meet the mark. These problems could be addressed by rule changes and stricter oversight.

Much of the overall increase in college attendance within

Georgia reflected redistribution of students across state bor-
ders; many who would have gone to college anyway simply
opted to remain in-state.[14] Other merit-based programs have
yielded 5–7 percent increases in total enrollment and could
be designed to yield more.[15] HOPE did little to boost college
attendance among students from low-income families because these students are much less likely to graduate from high
school and meet the criteria for support. But this is a limitation of any strategy based only on expanding opportunities for
the college-ready. Most merit-based aid, particularly that provided by private colleges, is aimed at the very best students; aid
based simply on achieving a B average comes close to targeting
the college-ready population.

The most serious shortcoming of the HOPE program—
and many of its imitators—lies in the funding structure. The
current program relies on a lottery that essentially taxes low-
income families at a higher rate than anyone else, exploiting
their ignorance of the low odds that they might win (see preceding chapter). The unfair redistributive effects are exempli-
fied by a study showing that the number of HOPE beneficiaries
increases car registrations in rich counties—apparently because
some parents induce their children to stay in-state by buying
them a car.[16] Funding such programs with progressive taxes
would obviously not prevent such gifts, but it would alleviate
the inequity of implicit taxpayer support for them.

RIGHTS, RESPONSIBILITIES, AND RECIPROCITY
When taxpayers finance the education of the younger generation, they expect payback in future years—the implicit inter-

generational exchange described in earlier chapters. Making the terms of this exchange more transparent could help build political support for major tax reform. Reciprocity can also take more immediate, direct forms, such as in the GI Bill providing benefits for veterans or civilian-service programs which would extend such possibilities for exchange. I favor a mandatory public service requirement for all college graduates, rather than one that simply helps students from low-income families pay their bills.

The original GI Bill was honest, straightforward, and generous. It reimbursed tuition costs at both public and private institutions and also paid a modest stipend to meet living expenses. Uncle Sam said, "Hey, you risked your life for us; now we're going to do whatever we can to help you get a college education." As World War II, and then the Korean War, receded into history, the number of veterans began to dwindle. In the Vietnam War era, the relationship between universities and the military reversed itself, as many young men headed for college in order to gain draft deferments. Still, many Vietnam vets made use of relatively generous provisions for college attendance.

But the armed forces, mindful of the high cost of its educational guarantees and moving toward a more focused system of volunteer recruitment, gradually changed the terms of its support for education, turning it into an increasingly complex and conditional job benefit that required commitment to payroll deductions and satisfaction of test score requirements in return for benefits with a strict ceiling. Military advertisements, such as "Join the army and earn up to $50,000 for college," were designed by marketing experts.

Many enlistees contributed $100 per month during the first twelve months of their tour, then either changed their minds, failed to qualify, or opted for two-year community college programs where the benefits were capped at less than $8,000.[17] Veterans' groups never enthusiastically endorsed the program.[18]

Not even the difficulty of finding volunteers for the exceptionally grueling and risky deployment to Iraq could override the business-oriented goal of minimizing short-term costs. In fact, some spokesmen for the armed forces explicitly argued that more generous benefits could discourage reenlistment.[19] When the Democrats won more congressional seats in the 2006 mid-term elections, however, veterans began to gain some traction. On his first day in office, newly elected senator James Webb (D) of Virginia filed legislation to restore the GI Bill to something resembling its former glory.[20] Within two years it survived a veto threat from President Bush and passed both the Senate and the House.

The federal government now guarantees veterans who served at least three months of active duty tuition assistance to public colleges in their home state, a stipend for books and supplies, and a housing allowance based on the cost of living in their area. Those who would prefer to attend a private college can apply for tuition waivers, with the federal government matching, dollar for dollar, any financial assistance they receive up to the amount of difference between the cost of attending the most expensive public university in the state and the cost of institution they aspire to attend.[21]

The new GI Bill is far less revolutionary than its predecessor because it provides for a group that is much smaller in both absolute and relative terms.[22] Nor is it likely to substantially increase enlistment. Top brass conceded as much when they announced in February 2009 that they will recruit skilled immigrants living in the United States with temporary visas, offering them the immediately valuable prize of citizenship. They expressed hopes that this outsourcing strategy could provide up to 14,000 recruits a year—a highly cost-effective strategy in the short run.[23] From a long-run perspective, it reminds one of the Roman Empire's desperate efforts to recruit foreign mercenaries.

The new GI Bill does provide a clear model for the development of a national service program that could create another route to reciprocity. During his campaign for the presidency in 2004, John Kerry proposed a "Service for College" initiative that would pay four years of public college tuition in exchange for two years of service (along with greatly expanded tax credits).[24] President Obama backed a similar service program during his campaign. On March 18, 2009, the House of Representatives voted to approve a huge expansion of federal support for public service, tripling the number of slots in AmeriCorps and creating new service programs focused on education, health care, and clean energy.[25] Volunteers will be eligible for an increased education stipend of $5,350—the same amount as a Pell Grant for 2009–2010. The new loan provisions described here also offer a powerful incentive for seeking employment in public service.

Some might argue that moving toward a model of service—whether military or nonmilitary—in return for education undermines the notion of public higher education as a right. We don't ask for service in return for elementary school and high school—we simply tax the beneficiaries of this educational investment. I agree with this criticism of service programs that are designed to increase access for low-income students and could even stigmatize those required to participate in them.

But a national service requirement for all college graduates could help them develop a more profound understanding of problems facing both our nation and the planet as a whole. Even students attending expensive private schools benefit from the tax exemptions these institutions enjoy (see chapter 6) and the availability of public financial aid and tax benefits. I believe that policies to expand public higher education should invoke principles of reciprocity and responsibility as well as rights.

AFFIRMATIVE ACTION AND DIVERSITY

Whatever funding mechanisms are adopted to increase access to higher education, college admissions policies will continue to shape the characteristics of the incoming class at the best institutions (see chapter 5). Private universities have considerable freedom to dispense aid to whomever they please. Public universities have come under increasing fire in recent years for efforts to apply affirmative action criteria for underrepresented minorities. A conservative Supreme Court has discouraged any explicit consideration of applicants' racial and ethnic characteristics, although its 2003 ruling in *Grutter v. Bollinger* instructed colleges to consider "workable, race-neutral alternatives" to achieving diversity.

Over the same period, political tensions, exacerbated by intensified competition for slots at top-ranked educational institutions, have driven increased reliance on standardized test scores for assessing student merit. Once established as a benchmark by rating services such as *U.S. News and World Report*, such test scores began to play an even more important role in admissions decisions. Yet considerable evidence suggests that class, race, and ethnicity have a bigger impact on standardized test scores than on actual school performance. As a result, many black and Hispanic students, some groups of Asian students, and low-income students, in general, play the admissions game on an unlevel playing field.[26]

Academic performance in high school should be given greater weight in college admissions decisions. Evidence for this argument comes from a fascinating policy shift in the University of Texas system in 1998. Forced by a legal ruling against affirmative action, the system both devised and publicized a race-neutral policy of promising admission to flagship institutions for all students who were ranked within the top 10 percent of their graduating class. Since regional and residential segregation within the state is pronounced, implementation of this rule both increased diversity and made it more difficult for high school students in the most affluent school districts to gain admission. Interestingly, the biggest benefits of the plan came from the publicity it received; the University of Texas had long given priority to applicants ranked in the top 10 percent.[27]

Representation of black and Hispanic students at flagship institutions in the University of Texas system probably remains well below the level it would have been if affirmative action efforts had not been quashed. But the program has increased racial/ethnic diversity to some extent, and it has certainly increased class diversity, bringing more residents of the state's relatively poor small towns and rural areas to the University of Texas at Austin (my alma mater—Hook 'em Horns!). Most heartening, and perhaps most significant in the long run, empirical analysis of the Texas experiment shows that graduation rates and other measures of achievement were not lowered by reliance on high school performance rather than test scores.[28]

The takeaway message here is that public universities in other states can improve diversity by following the Texas example and putting more emphasis on high school achievement than standardized test scores. Like the Georgia HOPE program, this approach rewards effort and achievement. While it does not level the playing field, it does something, at least, to reduce the tilt.

COMMUNITY COLLEGES AND ALTERNATIVE ROUTES

Not all high school students have the desire and ability to complete high school, much less attend college. We need to address this problem in every way we can and, in the meantime, improve the alternative opportunities that we provide the younger generation. Community colleges have long been seen as the bargain basement of the ivory tower. Because they serve a diverse population, including students who are working full-time or raising families, they are less successful than four-year institutions in moving students toward degrees. But their delivery of both academic and vocational training has expanded in recent years. Many of our police officers, emergency medical technicians, and health care workers are educated in these schools. And many students use community colleges as a stairway to the next floor of academic achievement.

New efforts incorporating research on student trajectories promise to improve community college advising and curricula. The Lumina Foundation's "Achieving the Dream" program aims to help low-income students and students of color complete courses and earn degrees.[29] The Bill and Melinda Gates Foundation recently committed funds to an effort to double the number of low-income students who complete a college degree or a certificate program within five years.[30] The Obama administration is building on these initiatives with a $2.5 billion state-federal incentive fund to improve performance.[31]

Georgia's HOPE program provides an interesting model here, offering significant support for students who do not meet the criteria for tuition subsidies at colleges and universities. These students enjoy free tuition and fees at vocational, non-degree-granting institutions as long as they complete their course work in a satisfactory way.[32] Other states are also expanding community college access. The state of Texas has established an impressive set of "early college schools."[33] Massachusetts governor Deval Patrick has proposed to make all fifteen community colleges in the state entirely free by 2015.[34]

Improved provision of high-quality distance and online learning programs could also help nontraditional students, including adults who are working full-time, gain educational credentials. The United Kingdom's Open University provides an excellent model of successful part-time distance learning, available to all at relatively low cost.[35] Based on principles of open access and equal opportunity rather than profit maximization, it receives high rankings for teaching excellence. British college students rank only one other institution in their country more highly—Cambridge University.[36]

When people can't find jobs, they need basic safety-net assistance as well as encouragement to gain new skills. Public assistance programs should reward—not punish—school attendance for individuals of all ages. Recent research shows that so-called welfare reforms introduced in 1996, including time limits and work requirements for receipt of public assistance, reduced both high school and college attendance among young adult women by more than 20 percent. Only states that supported schooling as an alternative to work reduced this negative impact.[37] Job training, retraining, and more training—along with more education in general—could help Americans cope with and hopefully bounce back from the Great Recession.

COMMON GOODS

Not everybody agrees that we have a moral commitment to provide equal opportunity to all. Libertarians roam the World Wide Web waiting to pounce upon and denounce anyone who makes this claim. But our social contract is not founded on ideals alone. It is also shaped by fundamental economic facts. We need social insurance. By pooling risk, we achieve a level of security we could never achieve on our own. By requiring that everyone participate, we can gain efficient protection from unanticipated problems. Bankers have long recognized this point, and, as recent bailouts attest, they rely heavily on the social insurance we provide.

Unfortunately, insurance can create problems of its own—overconfidence and bad behavior. That's why it requires careful design and democratic regulation. Opting out is a particularly serious problem. When economic inequality is high, the rich, the strong, and the healthy (and the privately educated) tend to form insurance societies of their own—gated communities that separate them from the rest of us yet rely on the services and subsidies we provide. They are sometimes able to use their power to off-load the risk—and the insurance premiums—on the rest of us. The huge bailouts of 2008 and 2009 dramatized their power.

Public investments in education are part of our intergenerational insurance system. We collectively invest in young people, and they promote the technological change and innovation that drives our economic system forward. They also collectively support us in our old age through their contributions to Social Security and Medicare. Overall, this system works pretty well. It improves equality of opportunity and rewards individuals for their talents and their efforts. It provides a safety net for both young and old, supplementing the role of family support and individual savings. If we continue to reduce our investment in public higher education, we will also lower future returns from the human capital that it creates.

Social insurance is not the only economic factor that

creates incentives for us to collaborate with one another rather than go it on our own. Growing problems of environmental degradation and climate instability urge us to end our obsession with the gross domestic product of things we buy and sell. The net financial wealth of the world is small compared to the value of ecological services produced by natural assets like our oceans.[38] Most of us in the United States work for a wage, but we devote about as much time overall to work on behalf of our families and communities.[39] The future itself represents part of the commons—something that we can all influence but no one can actually own.

State universities need to move away from the old business model based on minimizing costs and maximizing revenues toward a renewed commitment to the common good. Yes, that concept is hard to define, and that's why it offers such a magnificent challenge to our hearts and minds. We need to improve the quality of undergraduate education by paying closer attention to student engagement and successful graduation.[40] We need to improve our labor practices and stop relying on the exploitation of low-wage graduate student and adjunct faculty labor.[41] We need to reach out to the communities they serve and reclaim their mission to promote sustainable, healthy economic development.[42] We need to take the lead on important economic initiatives such as energy conservation and environmental sustainability.[43]

EXPANDING AND IMPROVING EDUCATION

In 1968, Martin Luther King Jr. gave a speech entitled "The Other America" in which he claimed that America practices

socialism for the rich and "rugged hard individualistic capitalism" for the poor.[44] Over the past year, the financial bailout
of banks and insurance companies deemed too big to fail has
vividly illustrated that claim. Our top-ranked private colleges
and universities also seem like socialism for the rich. Surely we
need to seek a better, more equitable balance between the pursuit of individual self-interest and principles of commitment to
the common good.

We need to explain the big picture and renegotiate all the
elements of the educational Big Deal. The United States has
long promised public education to children between the ages
of six and eighteen. The time has come to extend and improve
that promise at both ends—by providing high-quality early
childhood education for three- and four-year-olds and free
access to community colleges and public universities for those
who meet and maintain high academic standards. Why bring
toddlers into the plan? Because evidence suggests that early
investment in children's education improves their chances of
success in later years.[45] Without it, increased public provision
of higher education will offer only limited benefit to children
from low-income families.

Improvement in the quality of existing primary and secondary schools is also crucial. Public schools must be held accountable for student progress, along with efforts to train and
retain the best teachers. But public funding also requires struc-
tural reform. Class and race segregation, combined with dependence on local property taxes for school finance, contribute
to large disparities in high school graduation rates. Resource
disparities are overwhelming. In the fifty wealthiest suburban

school districts in the country, 16 percent of students are minorities and the median income is $120,000. In the fifty poorest urban school districts, 90 percent of students are minority and the median income is $19,000.[46] Many states, including California, Texas, and New Jersey, have experimented with methods of redistributing local tax revenues to less wealthy districts. The technical details are less important than the strategies for controlling political blowback by mobilizing support for principles of economic opportunity and demonstrating the public benefits of improved educational outcomes.[47]

Free public higher education is a viable goal. State university systems in California and New York once provided essentially free public higher education, and many other countries less affluent than us, including France, Germany, and Denmark, offer essentially free education and training today. In 2005–2006, the latest year for which data were available, about $41.8 billion was spent on tuition and fees at public degree-granting institutions in the United States.[48] If those costs were eliminated, more students would enroll, but existing infrastructure capacity—and strict admissions standards—would limit the increases. A conservative estimate of the total cost of eliminating tuition and fees would be about $80 billion a year in the near term—and that's not taking into account the reductions in loans and financial aid that would result.

Over the last ten years, political scientist and activist Adolph Reed Jr. has rallied students at many college campuses around demands for free public higher education, pointing out that the annual costs would not exceed expenditures on the Iraq war.[49] Many of the Democrats reaching for the 2008 presidential nomination offered schemes for lowering the cost of college. Dennis Kucinich presented the most straightforward proposal: rescind the Bush tax cuts for the rich to make higher education free.[50]

The political balance of power is now tipping in favor of more progressive taxation. State tax increases on the rich have recently been implemented in New Jersey and New York and are currently under consideration in many other states.[51] Tax increases on the top 1 percent of earners are a central aspect of the budget President Obama recently submitted to Congress, and are currently under discussion as a means of financing health care reforms.[52] A Gallup poll taken in November 2008 reported that 70 percent of Democrats, 60 percent of Independents, and a plurality of Republicans believe that high-income people pay less than their fair share of taxes.[53]

Individuals and families at the top of our income distribution have captured most of the gains from economic growth over the past thirty years. The education that many of them received at public expense often contributed to their economic success. They all benefit from the financial and social insurance systems that our country has put in place. They can afford to pay a larger share of the costs of public investments that serve the common good, and should be required to do so.

It will not be easy for higher education advocates to move away from scrutiny of their own institutions toward the ambitious goal of reforming larger budget and taxation policies. Many are already embroiled in turf wars over financial aid, or diversity, or student engagement, or student retention, or cost control, or another of a multitude of pressing concerns.

Divisions between private and public institutions and the rapidly growing for-profit sector are intensifying. In some ways, the disarray among advocates of higher education reform resembles that among advocates of health insurance reform before political resolve to move toward universal coverage had coalesced.

NEXT STEPS

Think of this book as Saving State U 101, an introductory course. The process of developing proposals to restructure public higher education finance will require attention to many details not covered here. Advocates will need to master both state and federal budgets and think carefully about ways of improving efficiency as well as equity. The process of mobilizing support for such proposals will demand formidable levels of creativity and commitment. We will need to get off the campus and into state capitals, looking for opportunities to form strategic coalitions.

And then there will be a final exam, a test in applied history and social sciences combined. Nobody knows exactly what will be on it, how survivors will be chosen, or what will happen to those who flunk. This book suggests how best to study for it. Don't rely on the standard textbook. Think about the big picture, the political economy of education, and the meaning of social democracy. Sharpen your pencils and back up your hard drives. Quit playing musical chairs and get ready for a momentous game of tug-of-war.

NOTES

Introduction

1. "Obama Calls for Better Data on Students and Urges Colleges to Control Costs," News Blog, *Chronicle of Higher Education*, March 10, 2009.
2. Estimate of cost of federal bailouts through April 30, 2009, from the *New York Times*; http://www.nytimes.com/interactive/2009/02/04/business/20090205-bailout-totals-graphic.html (accessed June 30, 2009).
3. Jeanne Sahadi, "Cost of Rescues: $835 Billion This Year," CNN, June 26, 2009, http://money.cnn.com/2009/06/26/news/economy/cbo_federal_budget_outlook/index.htm?postversion=2009062611 (accessed June 30, 2009).
4. State Higher Education Executive Officers (SHEEO), *State Higher Education Finance: Early Release, FY 2008,* http://www.sheeo.org/finance/shef/SHEF%20FY08%20Early%20Release%202.pdf (accessed March 21, 2009).
5. See studentdebtalert.org (accessed June 30, 2009).
6. National Center for Public Policy and Higher Education, *Measuring Up 2008*, Table 1, p. 8, http://measuringup2008.higheredu cation.org/print/NCPPHEMUNationalRpt.pdf (accessed August 4, 2009). Net college costs equal tuition, room, and board, minus financial aid.

1: The Big Deal

1. Evan Dobelle, "The Empty Pipeline," *Connection: New England's Journal of Higher Education*, Spring 2007, http://www.nebhe.org/content/view/209/128/ (accessed August 6, 2009).

2. See manuscript letter of Amherst to Bouquet, dated July 16, 1763, http://www.nativeweb.org/pages/legal/amherst/lord_jeff.html (accessed November 3, 2007).

3. Robert Costanza, Ralph d'Arge, Rudolf de Groot, Stephen Farber, Monica Grasso, Bruce Hannon, Karin Limburg, Shahid Naeem, Robert V.O. Neill, Jose Paruelo, Robert G. Raskin, Paul Sutton, and Marjan van den Belt, "The Value of the World's Ecosystem Services and Natural Capital," *Nature* 387 (May 1997): 253–60.

4. Robert Putnam, *Bowling Alone: The Collapse and Revival of American Community* (New York: Simon & Schuster, 2000).

5. John Maynard Keynes, "Economic Possibilities for Our Grandchildren," in *Essays in Persuasion* (New York: W.W. Norton, 1991).

6. Nancy Folbre, *Who Pays for the Kids? Gender and the Structures of Constraint* (New York: Routledge, 1994); Nancy Folbre, *Valuing Children: Rethinking the Economics of the Family* (Cambridge, MA: Harvard University Press, 2008).

7. T.W. Schultz, *Investment in Human Capital* (New York: Free Press, 1971); Gary S. Becker, *Human Capital: A Theoretical and Empirical Analysis, with Special Reference to Education* (Chicago: University of Chicago Press, 1964).

8. American Council on Education, "Poll Reveals Eight in Ten Voters Believe Vitality of America's Colleges and Universities Critical to Future Economic Success," press release, March 14, 2006, http://www.acenet.edu (accessed December 13, 2007).

9. In the 1950s, textbooks on public finance explained why some public services like education should be considered merit goods rather than merely public goods. See Richard Musgrave, *The Theory of Public Finance* (New York: McGraw-Hill, 1959), 13–15.

10. Gary Becker and Kevin Murphy, "The Family and the State," *Journal of Law and Economics* 31, no. 1 (1988): 1–18. On contractual solutions to common property problems, see Elinor Ostrom, "A Behavioral Approach to the Rational Choice Theory of Collective Action," *American Political Science Review* 92, no. 1 (1998): 1–22.

11. Peter H. Lindert, *Growing Public: Social Spending and Economic Growth Since the Eighteenth Century* (New York: Cambridge University Press, 2004), 103.

12. Ibid., 100.

13. Kenneth L. Sokoloff and Eric M. Zolt, "Inequality and Taxation: Evidence from the Americas on How Inequality May Influence Tax Institutions," *Tax Law Review* 59, no. 2 (2006): 167–241.

14. Robert Margo, *Race and Schooling in America* (Chicago: University of Chicago Press, 1994).

15. Michael Reich, *Racial Inequality: A Political-Economic Analysis* (Princeton, NJ: Princeton University Press, 1981); Edna Bonacich, "A Theory of Ethnic Antagonism: The Split Labor Market," *American Sociological Review* 37 (1972): 547–59.

16. Jonathan Teller-Elsberg, Nancy Folbre, and James Heintz, *Field Guide to the U.S. Economy* (New York: The New Press, 2006), Chart 5.3, p. 77.

17. Statistical Abstract of the United States 2007, Table 425.

18. Nancy Folbre, *Valuing Children*, Chapter 8.

19. See, for instance, Commission on National Investment in Higher Education, "Breaking the Social Contract: The Fiscal Crisis in Higher Education," 1997, http://www.rand.org/publications (accessed August 3, 2009).

2: The Sweet Boom

1. Craig L. LaMay, "Justin Smith Morrill and the Politics of the Land-Grant College Acts," 73–95, in *A Digital Gift to the Nation: Fulfilling the Promise of the Digital and Information Age*, ed. Lawrence K. Grossman and Newton N. Minnow (Washington, DC: Century Foundation, 2001).

2. Claudia Goldin, "The Human Capital Century and American Leadership: Virtues of the Past," *Journal of Economic History* 61, no. 2 (2001): 263–92.

3. John Dewey, "What Education Is," *School Journal* 54, no. 3 (January 16, 1897): 77–80.

4. Goldin, "The Human Capital Century"; Claudia Goldin and Lawrence F. Katz, "The Shaping of Higher Education: The Formative Years in the United States, 1890 to 1940," *Journal of Economic Perspectives* 13, no. 1 (1999): 37–62.

5. Peter Lindert, *Growing Public*, 106.

6. Goldin and Katz, "The Shaping of Higher Education," 53.

7. Ester Lowenthal, *The Ricardian Socialists* (New York: Longmans, Green, 1911), 98. See also Eileen Yeo, "Robert Owen and Radical Culture," in *Robert Owen, Prophet of the Poor*, ed. Sidney Pollard and John Salt (Lewisburg, PA: Bucknell University Press, 1971), 87.

8. Theda Skocpol, *Protecting Soldiers and Mothers: The Political Origins of Social Policy in the United States* (Cambridge, MA: Harvard University Press, 1992).

9. S.J. Kleinberg, *Widows and Orphans First: The Family Economy and Social Welfare Policy, 1880–1939* (Champaign: University of Illinois Press, 2006).

10. The original document is available online at http://www.teaching americanhistory.org/library/index.asp?document=607 (accessed July 16, 2007).

11. Claudia Goldin and Lawrence F. Katz, "Origins of State-Level Differences in the Public Provision of Higher Education: 1890–1940," *American Economic Review* 88, no. 2 (1998): 305.

12. Caroline Hoxby, "How the Changing Market Structure of U.S. Higher Education Explains College Tuition," National Bureau of Economic Research Working Paper No. 6323, December 1997.

13. Goldin and Katz, "The Shaping of Higher Education," 50.

14. Goldin and Katz, "Origins of State-Level Differences," 308.

15. Goldin, "Human Capital Century," 267.

16. Suzanne Mettler, *Soldiers to Citizens: The G.I. Bill and the Making of the Greatest Generation* (New York: Oxford University Press, 2005).

17. President's Commission on Higher Education, *Higher Education for American Democracy*, vol. 2 (New York: Harper, 1947), 23.

18. Joel Slemrod and Jon Bakija, *Taxing Ourselves: A Citizen's Guide to the Debate over Taxes,* 3rd ed. (Cambridge, MA: MIT Press, 2004), 17. Calculations for 2003 based on *2007 Statistical Abstract of the U.S.,* Tables 425, 464, and 648.

19. For a more detailed account, see Nancy Folbre, *Who Pays for the Kids? Gender and the Structures of Constraint* (New York: Routledge, 1994).

20. Lawrence Mishel, Jared Bernstein, and Sylvia Allegretto, Economic Policy Institute, *The State of Working America, 2006–2007* (Washington, DC: Economic Policy Institute, 2006), p. 33.

21. Nadine Cohodas, *The Band Played Dixie* (New York: Free Press, 1997).

22. E. Culpepper Clark, *The Schoolhouse Door: Segregation's Last Stand at the University of Alabama* (Birmingham, AL: Fire Ant Books, 2007).

23. Robert K. Fullinwider and Judith Lichtenberg, *Leveling the Playing Field: Justice, Politics, and College Admissions* (New York: Rowman & Littlefield, 2004).

24. Christopher Newfield, *Unmaking the Public University* (Cambridge, MA: Harvard University Press, 2008), 100. Newfield's account provides many fascinating details about the evolution of the California system.

25. Thomas Jefferson, Letter to Joseph C. Cabell, January 5, 1815, *The Writings of Thomas Jefferson* (New York: G.P. Putnam's Sons, 1898).

26. A. Clayton Spencer, "Policy Priorities and Political Realities," in *Condition of Access: Higher Education for Lower Income Students*, ed. Donald E. Heller (Westport, CT: American Council on Education and Praeger Publishers, 2002), 166.

3: The Slow Fizzle

1. State Higher Education Executive Officers press release, March 8, 2007.

2. William C. Symonds, "America the Uneducated," *BusinessWeek*, November 21, 2005; Richard D. Kahlenberg, *Left Behind: Unequal Opportunity in Higher Education* (New York: Century Foundation, 2004), available at www.fcf.org (accessed January 16, 2008). William G. Bowen, Martin A. Kurzweil, and Eugene M. Tobin, "From 'Bastions of Privilege' to 'Engines of Opportunity,'" *Chronicle of Higher Education* 51, no. 25 (February 25, 2005); Danette Gerald and Kati Haycock, *Engines of Inequality: Diminishing Equity in the Nation's Premier Public Universities* (Washington, DC: Education Trust, 2007).

3. Paul Krugman, *The Conscience of a Liberal* (New York: W.W. Norton, 2007).

4. James J. Duderstadt, *The View from the Helm: Leading the American University During an Era of Change* (Ann Arbor: University of Michigan Press, 2007), 145.

5. Christine Del Valle, "A Lot Less Moola Moola on Campus," *BusinessWeek,* October 5, 1992.

6. State Higher Education Executive Officers, *State Higher Education Finance,* Early Release, Fiscal 2008, http://www.sheeo.org/finance/shef/SHEF%20FY08%20Early%20Release%202.pdf (accessed July 1, 2009).

7. University of Massachusetts Amherst, All Funds Ongoing Sources of Revenue, Fiscal Year 2007, http://www.umass.edu/budget/updates/FY07/docs/table2.pdf (accessed August 6, 2007).

8. William C. Symonds, "Should Public Universities Behave Like Private Colleges? *BusinessWeek*, November 15, 2004, 97.

9. Michael S. McPherson and Morton Owen Schapiro, *The Student Aid Game* (Princeton, NJ: Princeton University Press, 1998).

10. The College Board, *Trends in College Pricing, 2008*, http://professionals.collegeboard.com/profdownload/trends-in-college-pricing-2008.pdf (accessed July 1, 2009).

11. C.C. Wei, L. Berkner, S. He, S. Lew, M. Cominole, and P. Siegel, *2007–08 National Postsecondary Student Aid Study: Student Financial Aid Estimates for 2007–08—First Look* (Washington, DC: National Center for Education Statistics, Institute of Education

Sciences, U.S. Department of Education, 2009), http://nces
.ed.gov/pubs2009/2009166.pdf (accessed July 1, 2009).

12. American Council on Education, *2007 Status Report on the Pell
Grant Program*, http://www.acenet.edu (accessed July 1, 2009).

13. Tom Mortenson, "It's Affordability, at Last," *Postsecondary Education Opportunity Newsletter*, October 3, 2006.

14. National Center for Public Policy and Higher Education, *Measuring Up 2008: The National Report Card on Higher Education*, http://
measuringup2008.highereducation.org/print/NCPPHEMU
NationalRpt.pdf (accessed July 1, 2009).

15. Joel Slemrod and Jon Bakija, *Taxing Ourselves: A Citizen's Guide to
the Debate Over Taxes*, 3rd ed. (Cambridge, MA: MIT Press), 18.

16. Detailed analysis is provided in a number of reports published
by the Center on Budget and Policy Priorities, http://www.cbpp
.org (accessed August 26, 2007).

17. See National Priorities Project, http://nationalpriorities.org (accessed September 15, 2007).

18. Fox Butterfield, "New Prisons Cast Shadow Over Higher Education," *New York Times*, April 12, 1995; Marcella Bombard-
ieri, "Colleges Trail Prisons in Funds," *Boston Globe*, November
25, 2004; *"Oregon: Spending on Prisons on Pace to Outstrip Education Outlays," Join Together*, April 23, 2007, http://www.join
together.org/news/headlnies/inthenes/2007/ (accessed August
26, 2007).

19. Chuck Collins, Mike Lapham, and Scott Klinger, "I Didn't Do
It Alone: Society's Contribution to Individual Wealth and Success," Responsible Wealth, August 2004, http://www.responsible
wealth.org/press/2004/notalonereportfinal.pdf (accessed August
26, 2007).

20. See, for instance, Kimberly Strassel, "Fat-Cat Cavalry Rides in to
Rescue High Taxes," *Wall Street Journal*, February 16, 2001.

21. Caroline M. Hoxby, "How the Changing Market Structure of
U.S. Higher Education Explains College Tuition," National
Bureau of Economic Research Working Paper 6323, December
1997, 8.

22. *Shaping the Future: The Economic Impact of Public Universities* (Washington, DC: National Association of State Universities, Office of Public Affairs, 2001), p. 38.

23. Committee on Policy Implications of International Graduate Students and Postdoctoral Scholars in the United States, Board on Higher Education and Workforce, "Executive Summary" *Policy Implications of International Graduate Students and Postdoctoral Scholars in the United States*, (Washington, DC: National Research Council, 2005), 1.

24. George Borjas, "Do Foreign Students Crowd Out Native Students from Graduate Programs?" National Bureau of Economic Research Working Paper 10349, March 2004.

25. Stephen Maguire, "Average Effective Corporate Tax Rates, 1959–2002," Congressional Research Service, Government and Finance Division, September 5, 2003; Robert McIntyre and T.D. Nguyen, *State Corporate Income Taxes, 2001–2003* (Washington, DC: Citizens for Tax Justice, 2005).

26. Robert Tannenwald, "Are State and Local Revenue Systems Becoming Obsolete?" *New England Economic Review* 4 (2001): 27–43; Melvin L. Burstein and Arthur J. Rolnick, "Congress Should End the Economic War for Sports and Other Businesses," *The Region*, June 1996, 35–36.

27. Institute on Taxation and Economic Policy, *State and Local Taxes Hit Poor and Middle Class Far Harder Than the Wealthy* (Washington, DC, January 2003), www.ctj.org/itep/ (accessed August 5, 2007).

28. Greg LeRoy, *The Great American Jobs Scam: Corporate Tax Dodging and the Myth of Job Creation* (San Francisco: Berrett-Koehler Publishers, 2005), 98.

29. See Tannenwald, "Are State and Local Revenue Systems Becoming Obsolete?"; Burstein and Rolnick, "Congress Should End the Economic War"; LeRoy, *Great American Jobs Scam*; Robert G. Lynch, *Rethinking Growth Strategies: How State and Local Taxes and Services Affect Economic Development* (Washington, DC: Economic Policy Institute, 2004).

30. Cost of tax expenditures from Massachusetts Budget and Policy Center, *Tax Expenditures and Economic Development* (Boston, MA: 2004), www.massbudget.org (accessed August 3, 2007), 9; governor's budget recommendation at http://www.mass.gov/bb/fy2004h1/budget_recommendations/govarea/heu.htm (accessed August 5, 2007).

31. Elissa Braunstein, *Tax Cuts and the Recession in the Massachusetts Fiscal Crisis*, Political Economic Research Institute, University of Massachusetts Amherst Research Brief 1, October 2003.

32. Massachusetts Budget and Policy Center, *Measuring Up: Taxes and Spending in Massachusetts, FY 2004*, November 2006, www.massbudget.org (accessed August 3, 2007), pp. i, ii.

33. Economic Policy Institute, *The State of Working America, 2008–2009*, Table 3.15, http:/www.stateofworkingamerica.org/tabfig/2008/03/SWA08_Wages_Table.3.15.pdf (accessed August 3, 2009).

34. Jonathan Teller-Elsberg, Nancy Folbre, and James Heintz, *Field Guide to the U.S. Economy* (New York: The New Press, 2006), 27, 28.

35. Paul A. Samuelson, "Where Ricardo and Mill Rebut and Confirm Arguments of Mainstream Economists Supporting Globalization," *Journal of Economic Perspectives* 18, no. 3 (2004): 135–46.

36. Alan S. Blinder, "Offshoring: The Next Industrial Revolution," *Foreign Affairs* 85, no. 2 (2006): 113–28.

37. Richard B. Freeman, "The Great Doubling: The Challenge of the New Global Labor Market," 55–65, in *Ending Poverty in America: How to Restore the American Dream*, ed. John Edwards, Marion Crain, and Arne L. Kalleberg (New York: The New Press, 2007), 60.

38. Thomas L. Friedman, *The World Is Flat: A Brief History of the Twenty-first Century* (New York: Farrar, Straus and Giroux, 2005), 237.

39. Friedman, *The World Is Flat*, 252, 253.

40. Milton Friedman, *Capitalism and Freedom* (Chicago: University of Chicago Press, 1962), 133; Milton Friedman, "The Social

Responsibility of Business Is to Increase Its Profits," *New York Times Magazine*, September 30, 1970.

41. Norman Matloff, "Debunking the Myth of a Desperate Software Labor Shortage," testimony to the U.S. House Judiciary Committee Subcommittee on Immigration, presented April 21, 1998, updated December 9, 2002, http://heather.cs.ucdavis.edu/itaa.real.html (accessed July 29, 2007).

42. Moira Herbst, "Outsourcing: How to Skirt the Law," *BusinessWeek*, June 22, 2007.

43. Steven Greenhouse, "I.B.M. Explores Shift of White-Collar Jobs Overseas," *New York Times*, July 22, 2003.

44. Tom Mortenson, "Class Segregation of Higher Education," May 24, 2006, http://postsecondaryopportunity.blogspot.com/ (accessed January 16, 2008).

45. Danette Gerald and Kati Haycock, *Engines of Inequality: Diminishing Equity in the Nation's Premier Public Universities* (Washington, DC: Education Trust, 2006), http://www2.edtrust.org/NR/rdonlyres/F755E80E-9431-45AF-B28E-653C612D503D/0/EnginesofInequality.pdf (accessed July 3, 2009).

4: Sticker Shocks

1. College Board, *2007–2008 College Costs Keep Rising: Prices in Perspective*, http://www.collegeboard.com/student/pay/add-it-up/4494.html (accessed July 10, 2009).

2. Price increases between 2006–2007 and 2007–2008 for both privates and publics were over 6 percent. Sustained over the four- or five-year period that it takes most students to graduate, this multiplies out to well over a 33 percent increase.

3. For more details, see PHENOM, "The Affordability Crisis in Massachusetts Public Higher Education," October 2007, http://phenomonline.org/documents/Affordability.pdf (accessed March 20, 2008).

4. This estimate is for 1999–2000 and includes loans and the cost of room and board for children living at home. Congressional

Budget Office, *Private and Public Contributions to Financing College Education* (Washington, DC: Congressional Budget Office, 2004).

5. Mark Lino, *Expenditures on Children by Families*, 2000 Annual Report, U.S. Department of Agriculture, Center for Nutrition Policy and Promotion. Miscellaneous Publication No. 1528–2000, 2001. This figure represents cumulative expenditures, without any discounting of the value of expenditures in different years.

6. Nancy Folbre, *Valuing Children: Rethinking the Economics of the Family* (Cambridge, MA: Harvard University Press, 2008).

7. Ibid., chap. 5.

8. Terri Cullen, "How Parents Can Help Children Pay for College," *Wall Street Journal*, March 3, 2004.

9. Many states do require divorced parents to contribute, prompting lawsuits complaining that no such requirements are imposed on parents in intact families. As of 1998, about twenty-one states authorized courts to bring consideration of college expenses into mandatory child support awards. See William V. Fabricius, Sanford L. Braver, and Kindra Deneau, "Divorced Parents' Financial Support of their Children's College Expenses," *Family Court Review*, 41 no. 2 (2003): 224–241. Existing rules make it very difficult for prospective students under the age of twenty-four to qualify as financially independent of their parents. Qualifying conditions include being an orphan or ward of the court until age eighteen or being a U.S. military veteran.

10. See Fin Aid, at www.finaid.org/otheraid/parentsrefuse/phtml (accessed July 30, 2004).

11. Charlene M. Kalenkoski, "Parent-Child Bargaining, Parental Transfers, and the Postsecondary Education Decision," manuscript, Center for Economic Studies, Bureau of the Census, Washington, DC, March 2002; Judith S. Wallerstein and Julia M. Lewis, *The Unexpected Legacy of Divorce: A 25-Year Landmark Study* (New York: Hyperion Press, 2000).

12. Tamar Lewin, "Easing a College Financial Aid Headache," *New York Times*, June 24, 2009.

13. General Accounting Office, *Student Aid and Tax Benefits*, GAO-02–751 (Washington, DC: General Accounting Office, 2002).

14. Susan M. Dynarksi and Judith E. Scott-Clayton, "The Cost of Complexity in Federal Student Aid: Lessons from Optimal Tax Theory and Behavioral Economics," *National Tax Journal* 59, no. 2 (2006): 319–56.

15. For instance, in 2004, a married couple with one college-age child, a fourteen-year-old, an income of $30,000 per year, and no assets was expected to contribute $1,064 per year (about 4 percent of their income), while the same family with an income of $60,000 was expected to pay $9,516 per year (about 16 percent of their income), and families with an income of $120,000 a year were expected to pay about $34,828, or about 29 percent of their income. Based on the calculator at apps.collegeboard.com, July 30, 2004.

16. Jane Bryant Quinn, "Helping Grandchildren Pay Their Tuition," *Washington Post*, May 28, 1995, H2.

17. Investment Company Institute, *Profile of Households Saving for College*, Fall 2003, 19, http://www.ici.org/pdf/rpt_03_college_ saving.pdf (accessed August 3, 2009).

18. T. Kane, *The Price of Admission: Rethinking How Americans Pay for College* (Washington, DC: Brookings Institution, 1999); D. Ellwood and T. Kane, "Who Is Getting a College Education? Family Background and the Growing Gaps in Enrollment," in *Securing the Future: Investing in Children from Birth to College*, ed. S. Danziger and J. Waldfogel (New York: Russell Sage, 2000).

19. *U.S. News and World Report, Ultimate College Guide 2008* (Naperville, IL: 2008), 136, 144.

20. College Board estimates for 2007–2008: Average private four-year colleges, $23,712; average public four-year colleges, $6,185; http://www.collegeboard.com/student/pay/add-it-up/4494 .html (accessed July 10, 2008).

21. Charles Clotfelter, *Buying the Best: Cost Escalation in Elite Higher Education* (Princeton, NJ: Princeton University Press, 1996).

22. William Bowen, Martin A. Kurzweil, Eugene M. Tobin, and Su-
    sanne C. Pichler, *Equity and Excellence in American Higher Education*
    (Charlottesville: University of Virginia Press, 2005).

23. American Association of University Professors, *2007–08 Report
    on the Economic Status of the Profession*, Table 4, http://www.aaup
    .org/NR/rdonlyres/3247B963-F66A-4E25-97A1-BDAA6E
    4E67C2/0/Tab4.pdf (accessed July 4, 2009).

24. Caroline M. Hoxby, "How the Changing Market Structure of
    U.S. Higher Education Explains College Tuition," National
    Bureau of Economic Research Working Paper 6323, December
    1997, 21.

25. Anthony Bianco, "The Dangerous Wealth of the Ivy League,"
    BusinessWeek, December 10, 2007.

26. Dan Clawson, personal communication, May 2009.

27. National Center for Education Statistics, *Digest of Education Statis-
    tics*, Table 231, http://nces.ed./gov/programs/digest/d06/tables/
    dt06_231.asp (accessed June 2, 2008).

28. Burton Fletcher, "Adjunct Instructors, the Burros of Academia,"
    January 30, 2003, http://www.chicagococal.org/news/Burros-of
    -Academia.htm (accessed July 10, 2009).

29. David Glenn, "Keep Adjuncts Away from Intro Courses, Report
    Says," *Chronicle of Higher Education*, April 4, 2008, http://chronicle
    .com/temp/reprint.php?id=s1wrbj0t0g37yb85hxmh8pzh073214
    pt (accessed June 2, 2008); see also Eric Bettinger and Bridget
    Terry Long, "Help or Hinder? Adjunct Professors and Student
    Outcomes," National Bureau of Economic Research Working
    Paper, May 2005.

30. Daniel Jacoby, "Effects of Part-Time Faculty Employment on
    Community College Graduation Rates," *Journal of Higher Educa-
    tion* 77, no. 6 (2006): 1081–103.

31. University of Massachusetts Office of Institutional Research,
    "Retention and Graduation Rates of Entering Full-Time First-
    Year Students, Fall 1998–Fall 2007," http://www.umass.edu/
    oapa/publications/factsheets/retention/FS_ret_03.pdf (accessed
    July 10, 2009).

32. Gordon C. Winston, "Subsidies, Hierarchy, and Peers: The Awkward Economics of Higher Education," *Journal of Economic Perspectives* 13, no. 1 (1999): 20.

33. Ibid.

34. "Williams: Where the Elite Get Eliter," *BusinessWeek*, April 28, 2003.

35. Total budget for 2008 of $457,781,869 from "University of Massachusetts Amherst: Base Budgets FY05 to FY08—General Operating Funds Only (State Appropriations, Tuition Retention, GOF, RTF)," October 15, 2007, http://www.umass.edu/budget/updates/FY08/docs/table1.pdf (accessed July 10, 2009); total full-time equivalent graduate and undergraduate students from "Instructional Service Matrix: Full-Time Equivalent (FTE) Instructed Students, Undergraduate and Graduate Combined, Fall Semester, 2007," http://www.umass.edu/oapa/publications/admission_enrollment_reports/fall07/enr3.pdf (accessed July 10, 2009).

36. Spreadsheet provided by David Murphy at UMass Amherst.

37. "The Endowment: Up, and Upheaval," *Harvard Magazine*, November/December 2007, http://harvardmagazine.com/2007/11/the-endowment-up-and-uph.html (accessed September 28, 2009).

38. Information on corporate tax rate in Massachusetts from Federation of Tax Administrators, "Range of State Corporate Income Tax Rates," January 1, 2008, http://www.taxadmin.org/fta/rate/corp_inc.html (accessed September 19, 2007); for Massachusetts higher education budgets, see Massachusetts Budget and Policy Center, "Comparisons of Past Year Spending," Budget Browser, http://browser.massbudget.org/CompareVersionsHistoric.aspx (accessed September 28, 2009).

39. Beth Healy and Steven Syre, "The Toll on Harvard," *Boston Globe*, December 4, 2008, http://www.boston.com/business/articles/2008/12/04/the_toll_on_harvard_81b/ (accessed July 4, 2009).

40. Mark Kantrowitz, "The Financial Value of a Higher Education," *NASFAA Journal of Student Financial Aid* 37, no. 1 (2007): 19–27.

41. Gary S. Becker and Kevin M. Murphy, "The Upside of Income Inequality," *The American*, May/June 2007, http://www.american.com/archive/2007/may-june-magazine-contents/the-upside-of-income-inequality/?searchterm=Becker%20Murphy%20upside%20inequality (accessed January 14, 2008).

42. Matthew Goldstein, "Chancellor's Address to the National Center for the Study of Collective Bargaining in Higher Education and the Professions," Thirty-fifth National Conference, April 7, 2008, http://www1.cuny.edu/forums/chancellor/?p=89 (accessed August 3, 2009).

43. Ibid.

44. National Center for Public Policy and Higher Education, *Losing Ground: A National Status Report on the Affordability of American Higher Education* (San Jose, CA: 2002), http://www.highereducation.org/reports/losing_ground/ar.shtml (accessed August 3, 2009).

45. Advisory Committee on Student Financial Assistance, *Mortgaging Our Future: How Financial Barriers to College Undercut America's Global Competitiveness* (Washington, DC: U.S. Department of Education, 2006).

5: The Pipelines

1. William G. Bowen and Derek Bok, *The Shape of the River: Long-Term Consequences of Considering Race in College and University Admissions* (Princeton, NJ: Princeton University Press, 2000); Douglas S. Massey and Camille Z. Charles, *The Source of the River: The Social Origins of Freshmen at America's Selective Colleges and Universities* (Princeton, NJ: Princeton University Press, 2002).

2. National Center for Public Policy and Higher Education, *Losing Ground,* 4.

3. Jennifer Cheeseman Day and Eric C. Newburger, "The Big Pay-off: Educational Attainment and Synthetic Estimates of Work-Life Earnings," *Current Population Reports* P23–210 (Washington, DC: U.S. Census Bureau, 2002).

4. See "Poll: 74 Percent of Americans Say Congress Out of Touch," CNN.com, October 18, 2006, http://www.cnn.com/2006/POLITICS/10/18/congress.poll/index.html (accessed June 7, 2008).

5. Frank Levy and Peter Temin, "Inequality and Institutions in Twentieth-Century America," Department of Economics, Massachusetts Institute of Technology, 2007, http://www.newamerica.net/files/Inequality%20May%201%20External.pdf (accessed June 5, 2008).

6. Isabel Sawhill and John E. Morton, *Economic Mobility: Is the American Dream Live and Well?* Pew Memorial Trust Working Paper, May 2007, http://www.economicmobility.org/assets/pdfs/EMP%20American%20Dream%20Report.pdf (accessed June 5, 2008).

7. Gary S. Becker and Kevin M. Murphy, "The Upside of Income Inequality," *The American*, May/June 2007, http://www.american.com/archive/2007/may-june-magazine-contents/the-upside-of-income-inequality/?searchterm=Becker%20Murphy%20upside%20inequality (accessed January 14, 2008).

8. Emmanuel Saez and Thomas Piketty, "Income Inequality in the United States, 1913–1998," *Quarterly Journal of Economics* 118, no. 1 (2003): 1–39. Tables and figures updated to 2005 downloadable in Excel format from http://elsa.berkeley.edu/~saez; Paul Krugman, "For Richer," *New York Times*, October 20, 2002.

9. Robert H. Frank and Philip J. Cook, *The Winner-Take-All Society* (New York: Penguin, 1995), 12.

10. Charles T. Clotfelter, "Demand for Undergraduate Education," 119–39 in *Economic Challenges in Higher Education*, ed. Charles T. Clotfelter, Ronald G. Ehrenberg, Malcolm Getz, and John J. Siegfried (Chicago: University of Chicago Press, 1991).

11. Robert Haveman and Kathryn Wilson, "Access, Matriculation, and Graduation," 17–43 in *Economic Inequality and Higher Education*, ed. Stacy Dickert-Conlin and Ross Rubenstein (New York: Russell Sage, 2007), 38.

12. Anthony P. Carnevale and Stephen J. Rose, "Socioeconomic Status, Race/Ethnicity, and Selective College Admissions," in *America's Untapped Resource: Low-Income Students in Higher Education*, ed. Richard D. Kahlenberg (New York: Century Foundation Press, 2004), 107.

13. Alexander Astin and Leticia Oseguear, "The Declining 'Equity' of Higher Education," *Review of Higher Education* 27, no. 3 (2004), 321–41.

14. Ronald G. Ehrenberg, "Reducing Inequality in Higher Education," 187–201 in *Economic Inequality and Higher Education*, ed. Stacy Dickert-Conlin and Ross Rubenstein (New York: Russell Sage, 2007); Tom Mortenson, "Class Segregation of Higher Education," May 26, 2006, www.postsecondaryopportunity .blogspot.com (accessed September 10, 2008).

15. M. McPherson and M. Shapiro, *Keeping College Affordable: Government and Educational Opportunity* (Washington, DC: Brookings Institution, 1991).

16. Danette Gerald and Kati Haycock, *Engines of Inequality: Diminishing Equity in the Nation's Premier Public Universities* (Washington, DC: The Education Trust, 2006), 4.

17. McPherson and Shapiro, *Keeping College Affordable*.

18. Paul Krugman, *Conscience of a Liberal*, 248, based on National Center for Education Statistics, *The Condition of Education 2003*, 47, http://nces.ed.gov/pubs2003/2003067.pdf (accessed August 3, 2009).

19. Nicholas Lemann, *The Big Test: The Secret History of the American Meritocracy* (New York: Farrar, Straus and Giroux, 2000).

20. James B. Conant, "Education for a Classless Society: The Jeffersonian Tradition," *Atlantic Monthly*, May 1940, 598.

21. Lemann, *The Big Test*.

22. Ibid.

23. Jerome Karabel, *The Chosen: The Hidden History of Admission and Exclusion at Harvard, Yale, and Princeton* (New York: Houghton Mifflin, 2005).

24. Ibid., 504.

25. Daniel Golden, *The Price of Admission: How America's Ruling Class Buys Its Way into Elite Colleges—and Who Gets Left Outside the Gates* (New York: Crown, 2006).

26. Karabel, *The Chosen*, 507.

27. "The Curse of Nepotism," *The Economist*, January 10, 2004.

28. Karabel, *The Chosen*, 551.

29. Richard D. Kahlenberg, *The Remedy: Class, Race and Affirmative Action* (New York: Basic, 1996); Gary Orfield and Edward Miller, eds., *Chilling Admissions: The Affirmative Action Crisis and the Search for Alternatives* (Cambridge: Harvard Civil Rights Project and Harvard Education Publishing Group, 1998).

30. Bowen and Bok, *Shape of the River*, 50, 288. See also discussion in Karabel, *The Chosen*, 538.

31. William G. Bowen, Martin A. Kurzweil, and Eugene M. Tobin, *Equity and Excellence in American Higher Education* (Charlottesville: University of Virginia Press, 2005).

32. William C. Symonds, "Campus Revolutionary," *BusinessWeek*, February 27, 2008, http://www.businessweek.com/print/magazine/content/06_09/b3973087.hym?chan=g (accessed June 8, 2008).

33. Justin Ewers, "Class Conscious," *U.S. News and World Report*, June 24, 2005, http://www.usnews.com/usnews/edu/articles/050502/college_print.htm (accessed June 9, 2008).

34. Ben Bernanke, "Remarks Before the Greater Omaha Chamber of Commerce," Omaha, NE, February 6, 2007, http://www.federalreserve.gov/BoardDocs/Speeches (accessed June 7, 2008).

35. Greg J. Duncan and Jeanne Brooks-Gunn, *Consequences of Growing Up Poor* (New York: Russell Sage, 1999).

36. George Borjas argues that the human capital of coethnics exercises an effect independent of parental human capital in "Ethnic Capital and Intergenerational Mobility," *Quarterly Journal of Economics* 107, no. 1 (1992): 125–50. See also his "Ethnicity, Neighborhoods, and

Human-Capital Externalities," *American Economic Review* (1995): 365–90; and William Darity, Arthur H. Goldsmith, and Jonathan R. Veum, "The Impact of Psychological and Human Capital on Wages," *Review of Black Political Economy* 26, no. 2 (1996): 13–46. On more general neighborhood effects, see Jeanne Brooks-Gunn, Greg J. Duncan, Pamela Kato Klebanov, and Naomi Sealand, "Do Neighborhoods Influence Child and Adolescent Development?" *American Journal of Sociology* 99, no. 2 (1993): 353–95. William Julius Wilson emphasizes the negative effects of persistent unemployment on the African American community in *The Truly Disadvantaged: The Inner City, the Underclass and Public Policy* (Chicago: University of Chicago Press, 1995).

37. Shelly J. Lundberg and Richard Starz, "Inequality and Race: Models and Policy," *Meritocracy and Economic Inequality*, ed. Kenneth Arrow, Samuel Bowles, Steven Durlauf (Princeton, NJ: Princeton University Press, 2000).

38. Quoted in Alexander Stille, "Grounded by an Income Gap," *New York Times*, December 15, 2001.

39. Gregory Clark, *A Farewell to Alms: A Brief History of the World* (Princeton, NJ: Princeton University Press, 2007).

40. Susan Mayer, *What Money Can't Buy: Family Income and Children's Life Chances* (Cambridge, MA: Harvard University Press, 1997); Charles Murray, "What's Wrong with Vocational School?" *Wall Street Journal*, January 17, 2007.

41. Robert H. Frank and Philip J. Cook, *The Winner-Take-All Society* (New York: Penguin, 1995).

42. Jack Hirshleifer, *The Dark Side of the Force: Economic Foundations of Conflict Theory* (New York: Cambridge University Press, 2001).

43. For a more detailed treatment, see the related discussion of Big Monkey and Little Monkey in Herbert Gintis, *Game Theory Evolving* (Princeton, NJ: Princeton University Press, 2000), 3–9.

44. Pew Research Center, "Trends in Political Values and Core Attitudes: 1987–2007," March 2007.

45. Tom Hertz, Tamara Jayasundera, Patrizio Piraino, Sibel Selcuk, Nicole Smith, and Alina Verashchagina, "The Inheritance of

Educational Inequality: International Comparisons and Fifty-Year Trends," *B.E. Journal of Economic Analysis and Policy* 7, no. 2, Article 10, http://www.bepress.com/bejeap/vol7/iss2/art10 (accessed June 7, 2008).

46. Sawhill and Morton, "Economic Mobility," 5.
47. Karabel, *The Chosen*, 5.

6: The Business Model

1. Rod Paige, "Letter to the Editor," *New Yorker*, October 6, 2003, 12.
2. Ernst Fehr and Simon Gachter, "Fairness and Retaliation: The Economics of Reciprocity," *Journal of Economic Perspectives* 14 (2000): 159–81.
3. Jeffrey A. Miron, "No Reason for State Universities," *Boston Business Journal*, July 13, 1992.
4. Gordon Winston, "Subsidies, Hierarchy, and Peers: The Awkward Economics of Higher Education," *Journal of Economic Perspectives* 13, no. 1 (1999): 13–36.
5. Available on line at Jamie Vollmer, http://www.jamievollmer.com/ (accessed July 2, 2009).
6. Larry Cuban, *The Blackboard and the Bottom Line: Why Schools Can't Be Businesses* (Cambridge, MA: Harvard University Press, 2004), 35.
7. For a review of this literature, see Paul Isely and Harinder Singh, "Do Higher Grades Lead to Favorable Student Evaluations," *Journal of Economic Education* 36, no. 1 (2005): 29–42.
8. Moira Herbst, "Oil CEOs: High Prices, Fat Paychecks," *BusinessWeek*, June 17, 2008, http://www.businessweek.com/investor/content/jun2008/pi20080616_449469.htm (accessed September 28, 2009).
9. Edward P. Lazear and Kathryn L. Shaw, "Personnel Economics: The Economist's View of Human Resources," *Journal of Economic Perspectives* 21, no. 4 (2007): 91–114.
10. Katherine Mangan, "Professors Question Texas A&M's Plan to

Award Bonuses Up to $10,000 Based on Student Evaluations," *Chronicle of Higher Education*, January 30, 2009.

11. B. Holmstrom and P. Milgrom, "The Firm as an Incentive System," *American Economic Review* 84, no. 4 (1994): 972–91.

12. Richard Rothstein, "The Corruption of School Accountability," *School Administrator*, June 2008, 14–18, http://www.epi.org/web features/viewpoints/rothstein-corruption_of_school_account ability.pdf (accessed August 14, 2008).

13. Tamar Lewin, "City to Track Why Students Leave School," *New York Times*, September 15, 2003.

14. David Figlio and Lawrence Getzler, "Accountability, Ability, and Disability: Gaming the System," National Bureau of Economic Research Working Paper 9307, November 2002.

15. Kian Ghazi, *Emerging Trends in the $670 Billion Education Market*, Lehman Brothers, March 17, 1997, 69.

16. "The University of Spam," *Chronicle of Higher Education*, June 25, 2004.

17. "Maxine Asher Has a Degree for You," *Chronicle of Higher Education*, June 25, 2004.

18. A summary of revenues for seven for-profit colleges in 2003 showed that all of them derived more than half their revenues from federal aids or loads. Corinthian College derived more than 80 percent of its revenue from these sources. See also "For-Profit Colleges Face New Scrutiny," *Chronicle of Higher Education*, May 14, 2004, 1.

19. Karen W. Arenson, "Report Calls for Tighter Rules on State's For-Profit Colleges," *New York Times*, May 22, 2006.

20. Goldie Blumenstyk, "U. of Phoenix Uses Pressure in Recruiting, Report Says," *Chronicle of Higher Education*, October 8, 2004; "Another Whistle-Blower Sounds Charges Against Kaplan's Higher-Education Division," *Chronicle of Higher Education*, August 7, 2008.

21. Daniel Golden and Matthew Rose, "Kaplan Transforms into Big Operator of Trade Schools, *Wall Street Journal*, November 7, 2003.

22. Karen W. Arenson, "Trade School Bent Rules to Get Aid, Officials Say," *New York Times*, July 23, 2007.

23. Garrett Ordower, "The Dot-Degree Boom," *The Nation*, March 28, 2006.

24. Edward Wyatt, "Investors See Room for Profit in the Demand for Education," *New York Times*, November 4, 1999.

25. Tom Robbins, "Bill Weld's School Daze," *Village Voice*, December 13, 2005.

26. Jessica Bruder, "Jolly Bill Weld Running Despite Wreck of Decker," *New York Observer*, December 4, 2005; Goldie Blumenstyk, "Company Managed by William Weld Is Investor in Troubled Trade Schools," *Chronicle of Higher Education*, September 2, 2005.

27. Jonathan D. Glater, "College Loans by States Face Fresh Scrutiny," *New York Times*, December 9, 2007.

28. David Cay Johnston, *Free Lunch: How the Wealthiest Americans Enrich Themselves at Government Expense and Stick You With the Bill* (New York: Portfolio Hardcover, 2007), 151–57; see also discussion in Charles R. Morris, *The Trillion Dollar Meltdown* (New York: Public Affairs, 2008), 147–49.

29. Sam Dillon, "Troubles Grow for a University Built on Profits," *New York Times*, February 11, 2007.

30. American Association of University Professors, *Where Are the Priorities? The Annual Report on the Economic Status of the Profession, 2007–08*, 16, http://www.aaup.org (accessed August 18, 2008).

31. Ronald G. Ehrenberg and Liang Zhang, "Do Tenured and Tenure-Track Faculty Matter?" National Bureau of Economic Research Working Paper No. W10695, August 2004.

32. Dan Clawson, "Tenure and the Future of the University," *Science* 324 (May 29, 2009): 1147–48.

33. Ellen Story, Michael Denning, and Eduardo Bustamante, "The Faculty Shortage at the University of Massachusetts Amherst," February 16, 2005, http://umassmsp.org/sites/umassmsp.org/files/facultydecline.pdf (accessed August 18, 2008).

34. *U.S. News and World Report, Ultimate College Guide 2008* (Naperville, IL: 2007).

35. For more information, see the National Survey of Student Engagement Web site at http://nsse.iub.edu/index.cfm.

36. Paul Fain, "High Pay Makes Headlines," *Chronicle of Higher Education*, November 24, 2006, http://chronicle.com/article/High-Pay-Makes-Headlines/13167/ (accessed August 3, 2009); Tamar Lewin, "Corporate Culture and Big Pay Come to Nonprofit Testing Service," *New York Times*, November 23, 2002, http://www.nytimes.com/2002/11/23/us/corporate-culture-and-big-pay-come-to-nonprofit-testing-service.html (accessed August 3, 2009).

37. David Kirp, *Shakespeare, Einstein, and the Bottom Line* (Cambridge, MA: Harvard University Press, 2004).

38. John L. Pulley, "Romancing the Brand," *Chronicle of Higher Education*, October 24, 2003; Thomas Bartless, "Your (Lame) Slogan Here," *Chronicle of Higher Education*, December 4, 2007.

39. American Council on Education, "Poll Reveals Eight in Ten Voters Believe Vitality of America's Colleges and Universities Critical to Future Economic Success," press release, March 14, 2006, http://www.acenet.edu (accessed December 13, 2007).

40. William Symonds, "Should Public Universities Behave Like Private Colleges," *BusinessWeek,* November 15, 2004.

41. Ginger Zhe Jin and Alexander Whalley, "The Power of Information: Do Rankings Affect the Public Finance of Higher Education?" manuscript, Department of Economics, University of Maryland, December 21, 2007.

42. Alan Finder, "Some Colleges to Drop Out of U.S. News Rankings," *New York Times*, June 21, 2007.

43. Jin and Whalley, "The Power of Information."

44. Memorandum to Department Chairs and Program Directors, College of Social and Behavioral Sciences from Robert S. Feldman, acting dean, re: Call for Proposals for FY2009 Amherst 250 Positions, August 4, 2008.

45. Steven L. Peck, "Science Suffers When Getting a Grant Becomes the Goal," *Chronicle of Higher Education*, October 10, 2008; Gina Kolata, "Grant System Leads Researchers to Play It Safe," *New York Times*, June 27, 2009.

46. Jennifer Washburn, *University, Inc.: The Corporate Corruption of Higher Education* (New York: Basic Books, 2005).

47. David Noble, *Digital Diploma Mills: The Automation of Higher Education* (New York: Monthly Review Press, 2003).

48. Jon E. Hilsenrath, "Behind Surging Productivity: The Service Sector Delivers," *Wall Street Journal*, November 7, 2003, A8.

49. National Education Association, *Advocate*, 25, no. 5 (Special Issue 2008), NEA Members in Higher Education.

50. Herbst, "Oil CEOs."

51. Patricia J. Gumport, "Academic Restructuring: Organizational Change and Institutional Imperatives," *Higher Education* 39 (2000): 76.

7: Fiscal Hell

1. Bert Waisanen, "The Property Tax Shuffle," *State Legislatures*, June 2007, 40–43.

2. Amy Finkelstein, "EZ Tax: Tax Salience and Tax Rates," manuscript, Department of Economics, MIT, and National Bureau of Economic Research, 2007.

3. Nancy Folbre, *Valuing Children: Rethinking the Economics of the Family* (Cambridge, MA: Harvard University Press, 2008).

4. Alberto Alesina and Edward L. Glaeser, *Fighting Poverty in the U.S. and Europe: A World of Difference* (Oxford: Oxford University Press, 2004).

5. Isaac Martin, *The Permanent Tax Revolt: How the Property Tax Transformed American Politics* (Stanford, CA: Stanford University Press, 2008).

6. Elizabeth A. Williams, *The Illusion of Local Aid: Extractive and Distribute Effects of the Massachusetts State Lottery on Cities and Towns*,

PhD dissertation, Department of Sociology, University of Massachusetts, Amherst, May 2000, 39.

7. Martin, *Permanent Tax Revolt*.

8. Nancy Folbre, *The Invisible Heart: Economics and Family Values* (New York: The New Press, 2001).

9. Charlie LeDuff and John M. Broder, "Schwarzenegger Tries to Add Some Substance to Celebrity," *New York Times*, August 21, 2003.

10. Laura Barrett, *Better Funding, Better Schools: A Roadmap to Overriding Proposition 2/12*, Massachusetts Teachers Association, 2002, www.massteacher.org (accessed December 18, 2008).

11. C. Eugene Steuerle, *Contemporary U.S. Tax Policy*, 2nd ed. (Washington, DC: Urban Institute Press, 2008), 166.

12. Carl Tubbesing and Vic Miller, "Our Fractured Fiscal System," *State Legislatures*, January 2007, 26–28.

13. Thomas J. Kane, Peter R. Orszag, and David L. Gunter, "State Fiscal Constraints and Higher Education Spending: The Role of Medicaid and the Business Cycle," Urban-Brookings Tax Policy Center, Discussion Paper 11, May 2003.

14. Elizabeth Winslow McAuliffe, "The State-Sponsored Lottery. A Failure of Policy and Ethics," *Public Integrity* 8, no. 4 (2006): 373.

15. Williams, *The Illusion of Local Aid*, 107.

16. Ibid.

17. Charles Clotfelter and Philip J. Cook, *Selling Hope: State Lotteries in America* (Cambridge, MA: Harvard University Press, 1989); Alicia Hansen, "State-Run Lotteries as a Form of Taxation," speech given at the National Coalition Against Legalized Gambling's Twelfth Annual Conference, October 8, 2005, www.tax foundation.org (accessed December 18, 2008).

18. *Statistical Abstract of the United States 2008*, Table 436.

19. Michele McNeil, "States Roll Dice on New Funding: Gambling Linked to School Aid in Fresh Wave of Ballot Measures," *Education Week*, October 15, 2008.

20. Global Insight, *Economic Impacts of Eliminating the Massachusetts*

State Income Tax, October 2008, www.masstaxpayer.org (accessed December 18, 2008).

21. See Tax foundation, www.taxfoundation.org.

22. For details on the Obama campaign tax plan, see http://www .barackobama.com/pdf/taxes/Tax_Plan_Facts_FINAL.pdf (accessed July 10, 2009).

23. For an account of this controversy, see Perry Bacon Jr., "Palin, Biden Clash on Taxes and Media," The Trail, *Washington Post* online, September 18, 2008, http://voices.washingtonpost.com/ the-trail/2008/09/18/palin_biden_clash_on_taxes_and.html (accessed December 20, 2008).

24. Thomas Frank, *What's the Matter with Kansas?* (New York: Henry Holt, 2004).

25. Larry M. Bartels, *Unequal Democracy: The Political Economy of the New Gilded Age* (New York: Russell Sage Foundation, 2008).

26. Christopher Newfield, *Unmaking the Public University: The Forty-Year Assault on the Middle Class* (Cambridge, MA: Harvard University Press, 2008). See also Bartels, *Unequal Democracy*.

27. Martin, *Permanent Tax Revolt*.

28. Ibid.

29. Massachusetts Taxpayers Foundation Bulletin, *2007 State Budget*, June 22, 2006, 4, www.masstaxpayers.org (accessed July 10, 2009); National Priorities Project, Cost of War Calculator, www .nationalpriorities.org (accessed July 5, 2009) (cumulative spending by Massachusetts taxpayers as of September 20, 2007, divided by the five years of war).

8: Saving Ourselves

1. Kelly Field, "Obama Pledges to Support Education, Urging All Americans to Get 'More Than a High-School Diploma,' *Chronicle of Higher Education,* February 25, 2009.

2. "Ivory-Towering Infernos," *The Economist*, December 13, 2008; Clare Cain Miller and Geraldine Fabrikant, "Beyond the Ivied

Halls, Endowments Suffer," *New York Times*, November 26, 2008; "How the Economic Downturn is Affecting Colleges: A Sampling," *Chronicle of Higher Education*, November 28, 2008.

3. Lisa W. Foderaro, "Public Colleges Get a Surge of Bargain-Hunters," *New York Times*, March 2, 2009.

4. Tamar Lewin, "State Colleges Also Face Cuts in Ambitions," *New York Times*, March 17, 2009.

5. Christina Couch, "Stimulus Gives Students Financial Boost," Yahoo! Finance, March 4, 2009, http://finance.yahoo.com/news/Stimulus-gives-students-brn-14538785.html (accessed March 16, 2009).

6. Thomas E. Petri, "Guaranteed Loans: Just Plain Expensive," *Chronicle Review*, June 22, 2007, B14; and Paul Basken, "Student-Aid Officers Struggle to Put Scandals Behind Them," *Chronicle of Higher Education*, July 20, 2007, A18.

7. David M. Herszenhorn, "Plan to Change Student Lending Sets Up a Fight," *New York Times*, April 13, 2009.

8. Candice Choi, "For Modest Earners, Relief Repaying Student Loans," *Associated Press*, June 28, 2009; Austin Wright, "New Loan-Repayment Program Allows Student Borrowers to Pay as They Earn," *Chronicle of Higher Education*, June 30, 2009.

9. Bruce Chapman, *Government Managing Risk: Income Contingent Loans for Social and Economic Progress* (New York: Routledge, 2006); Aaron Bernstein, "A British Solution to America's College Tuition Problem?" *BusinessWeek*, February 9, 2004.

10. Elaine Mag, David Mundel, Lois Rice, and Kim Rueben, "Subsidizing Tax and Education Through Tax and Spending Programs," Urban-Brookings Tax Policy Center No. 18, 2007, http://www3.brookings.edu/views/papers/lrice200705.pdf (accessed March 19, 2009).

11. Ben Elgin and Jessica Silver-Greenberg, "Scooping up the College Stimulus," *BusinessWeek,* March 23 and 30, 2009, 20–21.

12. Robert Ackerman, Martha Young, and Rodney Young, "A State-Supported, Merit-Based Scholarship Program that Works," *NASFAA Journal of Student Financial Aid* 35, no. 3 (2005): 21–34.

13. Christopher M. Cornell, Kung Hee Lee, and David B. Mustard, "Student Responses to Merit Scholarship Retention Rules," *Journal of Human Resources* 40, no. 4 (2005): 895–917; Matt Thompson, "The HOPE Scholarship and the Law of Unintended Consequences," 2005, http://www.educationlaw consortium.org/forum/2005/papers/thompson.pdf (accessed March 7, 2009).

14. Christopher Cornwell, David B. Mustard, and Deepa J. Sridhar, "The Enrollment Effects of Merit-Based Financial Aid: Evidence from Georgia's HOPE Program," *Journal of Labor Economics* 24, no. 4 (2006): 761–786.

15. Susan M. Dynarski, "The Consequences of Merit Aid," Working Paper No. RWP02–051, Kennedy School of Government, Harvard University, November 2002.

16. Christopher Cornwell and David B. Mustard, "Merit-Based College Scholarships and Car Sales," Working Paper, Department of Economics, University of Georgia, December 11, 2006.

17. Adolph L. Reed, "Majoring in Debt," *Progressive*, January 2004.

18. See Elizabeth Redden, "Best You Can Be Without a Degree," *Inside Higher Ed*, February 14, 2008, http://www.insidehighered.com/news/2008/02/14/veterans (accessed July 2, 2009).

19. Ibid.

20. See Elizabeth Redden, "Gauging the New GI Bill," *Inside Higher Ed*, June 20, 2008, http://www.insidehighered.com/news/2008/06/20/gibill (accessed July 2, 2009).

21. For a description of the benefits, see "Frequently Asked Questions," New GI Bill, http://www.newgibill.org/get_answers, and "The New GI Bill—Calculator," New GI Bill, http://www.newgibill.org/calculator (accessed September 25, 2009).

22. Milton Greenberg, "The New GI Bill is No Match for the Original," *Chronicle of Higher Education,* July 25, 2008.

23. Julia Preston, "U.S. Military Will Offer Path to Citizenship," *New York Times*, February 15, 2009.

24. Marc Porter Magee "National Service," *Blueprint Magazine*, July 25, 2004, http://www.dlc.org (accessed March 16, 2009).

25. David M. Herszenhorn, "House Passes Expansion of Programs for Service," *New York Times*, March 18, 1009.

26. Jerome Karabel, *The Chosen: The Hidden History of Admission and Exclusion at Harvard, Yale, and Princeton* (New York: Houghton Mifflin, 2005); Sigal Alon and Marta Tienda, "Diversity, Opportunity, and the Shifting Meritocracy in Higher Education," *American Sociological Review* 72 (2007): 487–511.

27. Mark C. Long, Victor B. Saenz, and Marta Tienda, "Policy Transparency and College Enrollment: Did the Texas Top 10% Law Broaden Access to the Public Flagships?" Working Paper, February 7, 2009, http://www.texastop10.princeton.edu/past_presentations.html (accessed March 19, 2009).

28. Alon and Tienda, "Diversity, Opportunity, and the Shifting Meritocracy."

29. See "Barrier Busters: Achieving the Dream Initiative Works on Many Fronts to Bolster Students' Success," *Lumina Foundation Focus*, Winter 2006, http://www.luminafoundation.org/publications/focus_archive/winter_2006/ATD_initiative.html (accessed March 15, 2009).

30. See "Gates Foundation Focuses on Community Colleges," *Community College Times*, November 13, 2008, http://www.communitycollegetimes.com/article.cfm?ArticleId=1317 (accessed March 17, 2009).

31. Timothy Smeeding, "President Obama and Antipoverty Policy: What Does the Stimulus Do to Fight Poverty, Educate Citizens, and Improve Public Health," *Fast Focus*, no. 2 (March 2009).

32. For a summary, see "Georgia's HOPE Scholarship," Terry College of Business at the University of Georgia, http://www.terry.edu/hope/gahope.html (accessed March 19, 2009).

33. For more information, see Texas Education Agency, "Early College High School Initiative," http://www.tea.state.tx.us/index3.aspx?id=4464 (accessed September 28, 2009).

34. Maria Sacchetti, "Patrick Seeks Free Two-Year State Colleges," *Boston Globe*, June 1, 2007.

35. See Open University Web site, "About the OU," http://www
.open.ac.uk/about/ou/p3.shtml (accessed July 2, 2009).

36. Alastair McCall and Zoe Thomas, "The Open University, *Sunday Times* (London), September 23, 2007.

37. Dhaval Dave, Nancy Reichman, and Hope Corman, "Effects of Welfare Reform on Educational Acquisition of Young Adult Women," National Bureau of Economic Research Working Paper 14466, November 2008.

38. Robert Costanza et al., "The Value of the World's Ecosystems Services and Natural Capital," *Nature* 387 (May 15, 1997): 253–60.

39. Calculations based on the American Time Use Survey: Bureau of Labor Statistics, "Table 1. Time Spent in Primary Activities (1) and Percent of the Civilian Population Engaging in Each Activity, Averages Per Day by Sex, 2008 Annual Averages," economic news release, U.S. Department of Labor, http://www.bls.gov/news.release/atus.t01.htm (accessed March 19, 2009).

40. See the National Survey of Student Engagement at http://nsse
.iub.edu/index.cfm (accessed March 15, 2009).

41. Dan Clawson, "Tenure and the Future of the University," *Science* 324 (May 29, 2009): 1147–48.

42. Gar Alperovitz, Steve Dubb, and Ted Howard, "The Next Wave: Building University Engagement for the 21st Century," *Good Society* 17, no. 2 (2008): 69–75.

43. For guidelines and examples, see the Sustainable Campus Web site at http://www.sustainablecampus.org/universities.html (accessed March 21, 2009).

44. Martin Luther King Jr. speech at Grosse Pointe High School, 1968, http://www.gphistorical.org/mlk/mlkspeech/mlk-gp-speech
.pdf (accessed March 21, 2009).

45. Nancy Folbre, "The Ultimate Growth Industry," Economix, *New York Times* blog, February 12, 2009, http://economix.blogs.
nytimes.com/2009/02/12/the-ultimate-growth-industry/ (accessed July 10, 2009).

46. Robert Balfanz, "Can the American High School Become an Avenue of Advancement for All? *Future of Children* 19, no. 1 (2009): 21.

47. For more discussion of this issue, see Nancy Folbre, *The Invisible Heart: Economics and Family Values* (New York: The New Press, 2001, chap. 6); see also Peter Sacks, *Tearing Down the Gates: Confronting the Class Divide in American Education* (Berkeley: University of California Press, 2007).

48. National Center for Education Statistics, "Table 350. Revenues of Public Degree-Granting Institutions, by Source of Revenue and Type of Institution: 2003–04, 2004–05, and 2005–06," *Digest of Education Statistics*, U.S. Department of Education, May 2008, http://nces.ed.gov/programs/digest/d08/tables/dt08_350.asp (accessed July 10, 2009).

49. Adolph L. Reed, "Majoring in Debt," *The Progressive*, January 2004; see also Laura McClure, "Higher Sights," Labor Party Press, May 2002, http://www.freehighered.org/h_lpp.html (accessed September 25, 2009).

50. Mark Dudzic and Adolph Reed Jr., "Free Higher Ed!" *The Nation*, February 5, 2004.

51. Confessore, "Taxes Not Seen as Making the Rich Flee."

52. See President Obama's FY 2010 budget at http://budget.senate.gov/democratic/statements/2009/Obama%20FY%202010%20Budget%20Brief%20Analysis_022709.pdf (accessed March 18, 2009); David M. Herszenhorn, "Leaders in House Seek to Tax Rich for Health Plan," *New York Times*, July 10, 2009.

53. Nimh, "Spread the Wealth? What Americans Think," Observationalism, November 1, 2008, http://observationalism.com/2008/11/01/spread-the-wealth-what-americans-think/ (accessed July 7, 2009).